Contra

Texas Poets Speak Out

Edited by

CHRISTOPHER MARTINEZ
&
MANUEL ROBERTO ORDUÑA

FlowerSong Press
McAllen, TX

Copyright © 2020 by Christopher Luis Martinez & Manuel Roberto Orduña
This book or any portion thereof may not be reproduced or used in any manner whatsoever without the express written permission of the individual authors, except for the use of brief quotations in a book review. The views and opinions expressed in this book do not necessarily represent that of FlowerSong Press, its owner or employees.

ISBN: 978-1-953447-76-0
Library of Congress Control Number: 2020947262

Published by FlowerSong Press
in the United States of America
www.flowersongpress.com

Set in ITC Berkley Oldstyle STD & Cambria

Cover design by Priscilla Dominguez

Forward by Manuel Roberto Orduña

Introduction by Christopher Luis Martinez

Edited by Christopher Luis Martinez & Manuel Roberto Orduña

Dedication

For every voice, heard and unheard

For the voters and the volunteers

For the activists and the allies

For the people

For the people

For the people

BUDDY WAKEFIELD • NAOMI SHIHAB NYE • EBONY STEWART • ANEL FLORES • ANDREA "VOCAB" SANDERSON • OCTAVIO QUINTANILLA • AMALIA ORTIZ • TARFIA FAIZULLAH • JOAQUIN ZIHUATANEJO • EMMY PÉREZ • GREGG BARRIOS • JOSHUA ROBBINS • NATASHA CARRIZOSA • SHEILA BLACK • BILL MORAN • VINCENT COOPER • VIKTORIA VALENZUELA • AMIR SAFI • GLORI B • AYOKUNLE FALOMO • M.R. "CHIBBI" ORDUNA • C.L. "ROOSTER" MARTINEZ • WENDY BARKER • GRIS MUÑOZ • SHERRIE "CANDY" ZANTEA • DANNY STRACK • LACEY ROOP • RODNEY GOMEZ • JOMAR VALENTIN • EDWARD VIDAURRE • ZACHARY CABALLERO • NATALIA TREVIÑO • ALEXANDRA VAN DE KAMP • KEVIN BURKE • TOVA CHARLES • SHAGGY • JOSHUA NGUYEN • ARIS KIAN • EDDIE VEGA • RYAN MCMASTERS • OMER AHMED • SARAH MADDUX • RJ WRIGHT • SIX GAWD • SIP • AXL • PAUL WILKINSON JR. •

Table of Contents

Forward ix
Introduction xi

The Voices of Texas Poets 1
We Muse 3

    Alexandra van de Kamp 4
    Aris Kian 7
    Amir Safi 9
    Sarah Maddux 12
    Ryan McMasters 13
    Wendy Barker 16
    Gregg Barrios 19
    Gris Muñoz 22
    Viktoria Valenzuela 24
    Ayokunle Falomo 25
    Tarfia Faizullah 29

We Disdain 33

    Lacey Roop 34
    Anel I. Flores 37
    Eddie Vega 42
    Joshua Nguyen 43
    Bill Moran 45

Jomar Valentin 54

Omer Ahmed 56

Joshua Robbins 57

Vincent Cooper 60

Edward Vidaurre 61

Joaquín Zihuatanejo 64

Octavio Quintanilla 66

Danny Strack 69

We Riot 75

Sip 76

Naomi Shihab Nye 77

M.R. "Chibbi" Orduña 79

Amalia Ortiz 84

Rodney Gomez 86

C.L. "Rooster" Martinez 88

Kevin Burke 91

Ebony Stewart 99

We Dream 101

Natalia Treviño 102

Six Gawd 103

Buddy Wakefield 105

Zachary F. Caballero 110

RJ Wright 113

Tova Charles 115

Emmy Pérez 117

Sherrie "Candy" Zantea 119
Ayokunle Falomo 120
Glori B. 123
Armando "AXL" Lopez 127
Paul Wilkinson Jr. 129
Natasha Carrizosa 131
Sheila Black 137
Vocab "Andrea" Sanderson 140
Sarah Maddux 141
Shaggy 144

Contributing Authors' Bios 147
Editors' Bios 164

FORWARD

To say that America is going through an unprecedented identity crisis is an understatement. A global pandemic. Economic recession. Record breaking unemployment. Mounting racial tensions. A refugee nightmare. White Nationalist mobilization. Ongoing protests. The effects of climate change increasing exponentially. An administration that ignores science and facts. A president unwilling to condone white supremacy or unify a country. But the job of a poet isn't new: we are charged with writing about the emotion of the moment, and a moment like this requires urgency. As an active performer in the spoken word circle across regional and national stages since the mid 2000's I am very familiar with the idea of using our voices to bring social injustices to light and provide a path for healing and growth. So, when Rooster came to me with the idea to put together an anthology of Texas voices reflecting and responding to the moment, the obvious answer was, "Hell yea!" We know that when people come together, we can affect change, but in 2016 only 46% of the voting age population in Texas turned out to vote, and only 42% in 2018. With the voter registration deadline only 2 weeks away, our activist instinct kicked into high gear.

We set to work creating a list of poets, both from the page and the stage, that we knew had something to contribute; had a history of fighting for social justice; the tenacity to speak up and speak out. We thought we'd send out the call and maybe half would respond with the interest and time to donate their work to the project. You can imagine our surprise when 95% answered with an enthusiastic yes! What we thought was originally going to be a small project with 10-20 contributors turned into this almost 200-page anthology with the work of nearly 50 writers from every corner of Texas, both past and present residents.

The true beauty of this book, and this country, is its diversity. Poets at every stage in their career, professionals and hobbyists, spanning decades in age, from so many cultural backgrounds and individual stories all saw the immediacy of the moment, and confirmed what we all knew to be true: together we can make a difference. Together, our voices will be heard. Every author, the editors, the publisher, all donated their time, work, and effort because we knew this wasn't about us; it was about making an impact.

      This book does not pretend to offer answers. Instead, it offers perspective. Personal introspection. Rallying cries. Rage and disgust. Hope and unity. We hope the work in this book captures this moment in time so that people understand the power they have in their voice; in their vote. I want to humbly thank everyone that helped in bringing this project to fruition, and I implore anyone reading this to see the truth every writer knows: your voice matters. Use it.

M.R. "Chibbi" Orduña
@gemineyes | www.gemineyespoetry.com
Spoken Word Artist, South Texas, 2020

INTRODUCTION

On a whim, the idea to put together this collection of writers came to fruition quickly thanks, in large part, to the incredible response from poets across Texas. Like the United States, Texas means different things to different people. For some, Texas is a source of pride--a land, people, and spirit, here long before the old world brought its violent kiss to the new world. For others, Texas is a microcosm of the United States--diversifying, inclusive, a site of hope and multicultural prosperity. For others still, it is a site of historical erasure and an oppressive reminder that counter-narratives are vital in fighting that erasure. Like the United States, Texas is vast with issues and concerns for the future, varying from region to region. And like the United States, our strength draws from the brilliant people within--the artists and poets; teachers and scientists; blue-collar, white-collar, no collar; rural and metropolitan; Fort Worth, Austin, El Paso, Corpus Christi, Houston, San Marcos, Dallas, Beaumont, Killeen, Waco, Bryan/College Station, Lubbock, Amarillo, Laredo, the Valley (Edinburg, McAllen, Harlingen, Brownsville, Weslaco, and others), San Antonio, and the many other towns and cities throughout.

For the editors, we love Texas and we fight for what we love. With this anthology, we hope to capture that fight and that love. CONTRA: TEXAS POETS SPEAK OUT is a collection of poetry from over 40+ writers from West, North, East, Central and South Texas. Edited by Rooster Martinez and Chibbi Orduña, CONTRA's mission is to: a) activate people to register to vote; b) activate people to GO VOTE; c) donate all profits from book sales to MOVE Texas; and, d) use art in direct opposition to fascism and anti-democracy.

The anthology is split in four parts: "We Muse", "We Disdain", "We Protest", and "We Dream." "We Muse" are poems of introspection and meditation. In this section, the authors ask questions of themself, what it means to be "American", and insights gained from such reflections. Viktoria Valenzula writes, in the poem, "Oh Say Can You See", "When I think of America my body aches / for something more protective than skin" (19-20). The powerful art of self-discovery is very much a political act. "We Disdain" is a section dedicated to the disgust and the rancor that the authors hold. In his poem, "Men, Women, and Children", Edward Vidaurre writes, "politicians / will always be turkeys, in any season. / prayers / are contrails against the vast expanse in the heavens, unheard" (7-10). These poems launch at the hypocrisy, loopholes, and cracks in the system that millions of Americans succumb to. "We Protest" is a section of poems for the fight, the rage, and the protest. In her song, "Demolish", Amalia Ortiz says, "Tear it down. Tear it down. Tear it Down. / We must unite to destroy the oppressive state" (6-7). A call to unified action for radical but necessary change. "We Dream" are pro-democracy poems; poems that hope; poems that believe a new, better, more inclusive American dream awaits. In the poem, "The Pledge," R.J. Wright says, "I do not pledge allegiance to the flag of the United States of America / Or any symbols created without me in mind / Instead I pledge allegiance to the things that bring joy and laughter / Like a toddler that wants me to watch them play" (1-4). The section rounds out the anthology as a testament to a better country.

In collaboration with Write Art Out, Flowersong Press, and Gemini Ink, Texas poets donated work that speaks to the times and struggles we're living in, the fears people are facing, the just activism fought in the streets, the importance of representation, a commitment to a pro-democracy nation, and hope for the future. For that, we'd like to thank all the poets, poetry friends, family, and fans who believe in this project and gave their time, art, and energy to it. We'd like to thank Flowersong Press for immediately jumping on the project without hesitation. We'd also like to thank Alexandra van de Kamp and Gemini Ink for their resources and help. And lastly, we'd like to specifically thank Priscilla Dominguez for creating the cover and design of the book, and Julia Orduña for helping to organize the virtual show.

Additionally, we'd like to show appreciation to the volunteers and behind the scenes community leaders for putting in countless hours and miles upon themselves activating others to vote and to get involved in the political process. We'd like to thank MOVE Texas for the work they do and all other grassroots pro-democracy organizations across the country as well. We'd like to thank the activists out in communities and schools 24/7/365-- you are the spirit of change doing the hard work, mil gracias. We'd like to thank the many different communities from which we come from, the mentors we've had along the way, and the support of friends and family.

As much as this book is *contra/"against"* the corrupt, unjust, violent and brutal days facing people in America, it is still an anthology of hope. In the poem, "Propriety (take two)", Naomi Shihab Nye says, "We are voting for ourselves" (7). The people/la gente ultimately decide how this world moves forward or doesn't. We need to take the dream back. We need a new dream. We need words and ideas that might save our souls, our land, and our people. And by "our people", we mean anybody who toils in all 50 states and US territories. May art be a fulcrum for change in the hearts of Texans and people *across* the United States. As much as we wish this book was a brick, we're thankful it isn't. And though it may not be a weapon or a fist, it is pages and pages of fight.

Lastly, we'd like to thank you, the reader. Thank you for your support. Sit with these words and be open to the possibility of change through art and redefining the dream of *America*.

Viva La Lucha

Black Lives Matter

Intersectional Feminism is the Wave

Love is Love

Trans Rights are Human Rights

No One is Illegal on Stolen Land

Editors:

C.L. "Rooster" Martinez
@ayoroost IG/Twitter
Poet, San Antonio, Texas

The Voices of Texas Poets

2.. Contra

Texas Poets Speak Out 3

We Muse

School shootings prove that

lawmakers fail every time

a student passes

Eddie Vega

ALEXANDRA VAN DE KAMP

The November Poem

November is giving me the finger today
but delicately, as in the leaves are all the color of cold coffee,
as in the sheriff in the TV series I've been watching
is slowly losing his even-keeled perspective--
a calm, well-thought-through approach to the

crimes of his Wyoming county. Snow
sniffs its way into the occasional scene, but mostly
we are on a New Mexico set with chili peppers hanging
from rafters and Margaritas flashing their neon greens.

Did I say I was trying to write about November—always
the foggy head-cold of autumn? Let me inhale the secondhand smoke
of my nation and not mind how car commercials drive
their pearl-tinted vehicles down impossible night roads.

Let me assert a promise is a missed rose of light, something blooming
off to the side of the throat-spittle and crushed lives, the headlines
tipsy with their syllables, the tweet fuming in its cage of characters—
what we all find ourselves mesmerized by, despite the best

of intentions. And all I wanted was to write a poem laced
with its own quiet attentiveness.

This is Not a Fever

with its lava lamps of perspiration, its
blackening April skies.

This is not my husband's dream
where he moves in with friends, bumps into
a female acquaintance as an odorless
contagion circles the neighborhood.

This is not a contagion
        of unwritten poems
        of trees
        of words like *mask* and *expertise*
        of thwarted murder plots
        of negligees of doubt

This is not a group of small gray birds
that arrowed just now through the sky,
slashing past my upraised hand.

This is not a hand—tender collection of five
digits—eager beast we carry at the ends
of our arms; how we try and try.

I would rather not morph into
a statistic, by the way, with its
specific yet vague reckoning, its
daily finger-tap of grief
and hope; its relentless messaging.

But I am this poem with a metronome
tucked deep inside—an invisible
tick-tock as the day
stacks the fog, like shredded data
into the wet
green of the trees.

This is not a Caribbean island—its
rum daiquiris and sand-covered

6.. Contra

eyelashes, its button-sized

jelly fish seeping through
the blue of my swimming suit.

This is not their stings rising out of my skin
a week later—tender necklace
I carried on my reddened chest.

This is not an 8AM headline
with sniffling *the's* and not-

fully-tested drugs, its *these*
and *those* sidling past

the dead bodies.
The clouds

have frayed cuffs, the street
is a waiting mouth, the

murder rate goes up or down
in direct proportion

to the number of people
gathering together.

Pollen falls, powders our cars; children
tangle in their own voices.

ARIS KIAN

Can a Body Be

Can a body be a barrier? Dare itself to sit
at the edge of our daunting cliff
without jumping? Can it find a new home

within the risk? With the awkward and unsure?
Can it bend in uncertainty for the bodies
they've watched break over and over?

To my white friends sending
their deepest condolences from the comfort
of a comment section: I've watched

a cloud of tear gas tear through a crowd
quicker than a prayer. Are your thoughts
with me, in the safety behind a screen,

or at the dinner table with your kin
burying my Black life beneath All?
Can it catch the rubber pellets

of the devil's advocate? Can it correct?
Can it call out? Can it be a coating of armor,
collecting dust and rubble, a Kevlar vest color

of stripe and fifty stars? Can it barricade,
can it block? Can it be the breathing thing
between my teeth and the pavement?

Can it swallow the sun? Make a midnight
for all those underground to come up for air
and continue the work unspotted?

Can it spit out again and again, a sun here,
a son there, a lost light for every mother
left holding wind empty in her hands?

8.. Contra

Can it windmill? Can it wind up? Can it war cry
without handing over its tears as its only
sacrifice? Can it suffice as is? Can it speak

without speaking for? Without speaking over?
Can it ask questions into a search bar
instead of a sobbing mouth? Can it lose count?

Can it run its hands over unfamiliar names
and feel the edges of a father, a spouse,
a subtle smile on a shared sidewalk?

Can it swivel sticks between its palms?
Until the blisters peel? Can it blow until it sparks?

Until it starts a fire, and know, that whatever
burns down was already broken?

Amir Safi

American Dreaming

Can you tell me what an American looks like?
Has anyone ever asked you where you're from?

When you answered *from here*.
Did they ask you again as if you misunderstood the question?

A Muslim boy tells me that he dreams
of being president of the United States.

Why is Donald Trump so uncomfortable?

We all know what happens when the American flag hits the floor
stained, soiled, and tattered.

But what happens when your people hit the floor?
stained, soiled, and tattooed.

Will you be there to pick them up,
when they are hanging at half-mast?

How does the term Arab Christian make you feel?
An Arab Christian said God is Great,
the same Arab Christian said Allahuakbar
— do you fear any different?

What's wrong America?
Are you afraid you'll catch the Islam?

I know America is a nation founded by great men
because it has a hard time apologizing.

At this point you may be thinking, *if he doesn't like it here —
why doesn't he just go back home!?*

I have an answer for that. I was born in Ames, Iowa. And I will not go back there until they publicly apologize for allowing Michele Bachmann to win the Ames Straw Poll in 2011. It's embarrassing.

10 .... Contra

Others may be thinking,
This guy clearly hates Americans.

And I would ask you, *How can I hate myself?*
How can I hate my American little brother?
I remember when my father earned his citizenship after living here for over 25 years, they gave him two tiny American flags that day and he held them as proudly as he held his two American boys.

My best friends are Americans.
I found them in a box of crayons,
but the best food I've had is from restaurants,
where they don't speak a word of English.

America, it is easy to forget where you are from, when are from everywhere.

Yet still, we have an immigration policy that keeps my family apart because it's designed
to keep people who look like me out.

Yet still, my father came here at 17 years old,
not speaking a word of English.

You Cannot Dig Your Heels in Deeper Than a Child's Grave

Emma, as in
the German word *ermen,* meaning:
whole universe. Emma, as in
novel written, showcasing a
heroine no one is supposed to
like. Emma, as in Lazarus, as in
inscribed in bronze, as in red
brass, as in gun metal. Lazarus, as
in canonized, as in the
resurrection of somebody's son.
Gonzalez, as in the son of
Gonzalo, as in the Spanish word
meaning: *battle,* as in the Battle
of Gonzales, as in
come and take it.
And here she
comes,
new colossus girl
all brown and buzz cut
the heroine they do not like
the whole universe their wall
could not protect them from
both the cannon and the taking.

Sarah Maddux

Three

One of the treatments used during the COVID-19 outbreak
Is the hundred-year-old practice of blood plasma transfusion
Blood serum is taken from disease survivors,
With all their virus battling antibodies
And infused into those still fighting for their lives

And isn't that the most potent type of healing?
When those of us who have made it through the dark
Have staggered out of the tunnel
Still bleeding and gasping for air
Reach back
And grasp the hands of those still trying to find the light?

The R0 is the average number of people to which an infected
Person will pass the disease
For COVID-19, that number is about 3
The approximate number of people a single survivor's
Antibodies can treat is also 3

Which is to say
That we all have as much capacity to heal
As to hurt

Ryan McMasters

Death Count

When the Coronavirus cases surged in May my sister blamed it on the protests—where basically everyone but the cops wore masks & gave effort in maintaining social distance. I focused on the beach goers—where weeks before, they were riddling the sand with unmasked bodies laughing in the face of a virus that doesn't see privilege.

We went on a walk in April, her talking about the patience we should have for our president, how companies are using their resources & using them to create more hand sanitizers & masks, & I mention that Trump disbanded the National Security Council in 2018 for a situation just like this.

"Dad would've voted for Trump again. Sorry."
She could've said nothing, like many times before & it slipped out, like the sorry was intended for anything other than its definition.

I don't know what apologies are anymore.
Words are a sickness family uses to force you to remember.

This presidency has shown me what I am,
what I stand for,
who I'm willing to invest in,
who I'm surrounded by,
how my family are good people,
but will actively vote against my interests,
my livelihood,
will vote for a world that will make me less safe, that will not protect me,

but they love me so/ much,
they support/ me,
as long as the gay/ isn't frothing from my rabid, sewer mouth.

Hooray. I no longer live in a closet but swept under a rug with all the other unclaimed dust. What a perspective to gather all the crumbs, thankful I am not dead, but unable to thrive.

During a local election, I drove my father to the voting booths. I read the ballot as his proxy. We conversed about immigration while he drove us home. He said my thoughts made sense but were idealistic like it's unattainable because everybody says it is. I was a good son then. I am a good son now.

I am not happy that my dad is dead, but I am not sad that his vote won't be included in this voting cycle.

I am his legacy–
his energy stoked while carrying it along a different path,
a new era,

away

from the rest of my family,

away

from this presidency.

Convenience Remorse

Candles can be lit in my house now.

My dad was sensitive to smoke so anything lit could cause a nasal infection.

His Fox News shows were one of the first things to be cleaned off the recording schedule in the Spring.

He always put passion into politics, how he respected my right to vote & how proud he was that I took voting so seriously, even if he knew he would cancel what I submitted in the ballot box with what he did in his.

He had a growing stack of books that went bad around the time his eyesight did, so rather than burning them, I recycled them. I didn't believe the message on the pages, but I will always believe in paper.

Without his diet influencing our eating habits, our menu has changed deliciously. No more cardboard for dinner.

My dad has a computer room with storehoused papers dating back 20+ years. My mom was given the ok to shred everything once he was gone. She's wanted to do this for decades. This, her post-mortem party, turning foreign memories into confetti.

How horrible these fringe benefits plague my mind as I grieve the loss of my father. Understand that grief is a shapeshifter, an ink-stained fingerprint: one day you break, another, you resolve at a disturbing pace. None of it is wrong.

Concern is a fixation when I am not finishing a task.

I do nothing for a day after a month and a half of doing something & I have a headache, pulsating like an alarm clock. I want to light a candle & the lighter is broken. I eat barbecue as an indulgence & I'm sick to my stomach. Am I a monster for moving on too quickly? Am I making a cage from all the silver linings I've collected to cope with his death?

WENDY BARKER

Driving While White

Tarantula eyelashes in my twenties, fluttering
above a miniskirt. And the seraphic smile I'd
give the cop who'd pulled me over, speeding.
Again. The time I was hitting 80 in a 60 mph
zone, and lowered my eyelids, bent my head
to the officer, confessing I'd just learned I was
pregnant, so happy I didn't even notice I was
speeding, and he grinned, "You be careful now,
little lady." Dozens of times: "Oh, officer, I'm
so sorry! I just didn't realize!" "Oh my gosh,
I'll slow down, I promise." And the response:
always a kindly "You do that, ma'am." These
days, still blue-eyed, no longer blond, silver-
haired, I'm a nice old white lady, and when
my bike-tanned husband is driving, I will
lean across him, tilt my head, smile, gush
to the cop who stopped us. Never ticketed.
In the sixties, when I asked my Black lover
why not get married, I wanted his babies, he
said, "You don't know how hard it could get."

Cockroaches

Phoenix in the fifties, and my British-bred
square-shouldered mother smashing roaches
with a fury that, even as a kid, I knew must
have come from somewhere else and long
ago, as she fumed against the filthy creatures
invading her spotless house. These insects do,
of course, spread germs, will invade your nose
or ears while you're sleeping. And now my own
house crawls with the damned pests, so I smash
them every chance I get, flushing their carcasses
down the toilet. But what is this new anger that
engulfs me now? With their tough exoskeletons,
spindly antennae, they skitter across floors and
counters, into the room where the TV blares
reports of more gunshots, more Black killings
by white cops, knees on necks, choke holds
blocking blood to the brain. The police are
protected by their own kinds of exoskeletons,
riot gear, helmets, chest shields, as they taser,
pummel, and shoot. I've read that cockroaches
wriggled onto slave ships leaving West Africa
and packed with kidnapped, naked, branded
women, toddlers, men. The insects gobbled
food and multiplied as they slithered over
bodies crammed on planks, covered in shit,
piss, gasping for clean air. So roaches reached

18.. Contra

our own shores, rampant ever since. And I

know my mother, shipped alone from England

as a teen (though sailing first class all the way),

would—if she were alive today—join me in

pounding the soles of our shoes onto every

roach we spotted. My own anger is not enough.

GREGG BARRIOS

La Virgen Guadalupe has no Papers

her bronze skin makes her suspect
and hell, no green card as well
la migra began raids downtown
where raza works and plays
hide-and-seek a jale if you dare
blame ICE's Operation Jobs
a lame way to sanction mobs
bent on scaring workers away
only coyotes worked today.

I heard talk in the poolroom
About shakedowns at dawn
obreros arrived at the plants
los perros swarmed like ants.
I wanted to run away from SA
donde mi gente strives to be brave
"Stay inside. You might be next!"
niños in school trying to stay cool
recite, "hay plesha lichens to di flac."

La migra won't be fooled by Spurs
mania running scared into churches
empty today, barrio bakers gave
stale bolillos to the hungry today.
The end must be near abuelita said
as votives to our Lady flickered away.
El pueblo can't celebrate las fiestas
patrias if they're rounding up raza
in la plaza Dieciséis, ain't no way.

They're taking la guadalupana away
man, she wasn't a legal resident, you see
they raided shelters, arrested protesters

our mother struggled and fought to be free.
Watch it! She doesn't speak ingles, your way!
out over the clash, what's that she says?
"Know your rights, stand proud, don't bend!"
Or, was it? "Los rinches son pinches también,"
No sé, but she wasn't joking. Amen.

Advertisement for Chicano Unity

Forget envy. We are nothing without each other.

Respect everyone. Even the least of us has need for pride.

Respect the religion of our people. It sustains us in ways we sometimes forget or don't understand.

Do not take or borrow that which you will not return.

To accept from institutions creates lust for money and promises of lies.

Our leaders must hold high ideals above high positions.

If you do not experience the oppression of jail, false arrest or a life of stooping on your knees, you cannot feel our people's anguish or pain.

Past injustices cannot be corrected retroactively. To fail to see this permanently divides our goals. Don't look back. Look forward.

Don't fall prey to the form game. You are not a Title 1 or Migrant. You are you and down with the damn name game.

A candidate's victory is unity of our goals not a self-centered hollow hurrah.

Be aware. Know what discrimination is. Paranoia can keep you awake. But know the real from the fake.

To assimilate is to assume.

As long as our culture lives, we will continue to survive.

Gris Muñoz

Americans

"Come here, Mija, I want you to see where you come from," he says, and leads me to a dusty picture frame hammered onto his bedroom wall, arranged next to an array of grainy mementos and army photos. In it is a faded newspaper clipping from 1954. The frames have been there for years, but I can't recall ever really noticing this particular one. It shows a group of farmworkers standing in line, all of them holding onto sacks, their hands clasped around the thinnest part, the bulk dragging on the ground. Every person in the photograph is wearing jeans and wide-brimmed sombreros. Some of them are children. They're standing next to a tractor trailer, the sky and clouds vast around them.

The caption reads, "In this 1954 photo, pickers weigh their sacks filled with cotton. The trailer was headed to the gin to be processed."

"That's us," he says proudly. "My mom and dad and us all together, piscando algodón en el rancho." Their names are not in the caption, but as I look closer, I see my father's tiny child's face, his features defiant even then, his striking eyes gazing upwards.

"Dad, what year were you born? You were just a little boy here."

"I was born in 1945. I was nine years old in that picture. We would follow the pisca by the seasons, New Mexico, Arizona, California. It didn't feel like labor then, even though I would get tired. We would get to travel. Your grandma was happiest when we were in Arizona, where she was born, her and her mother. Her mother, your great-grandmother was full-blood Apache, and I think something about being on that land made grandma Mague feel stronger. Those are some of the best memories I have of my mother and father, of your Tio Lencho that passed. All of us worked, Mija, but we were Americans, too. When I turned sixty-five and went down to the Social Security office, the teller said, 'Mr. Muñoz, it shows here you've been contributing to Social Security since you were nine years old.'"

I can't exactly express it, but at that moment, I feel shame as I picture myself at nine, riding my bike or roller skates down the sidewalk in front of the only home I ever had to know. When I got my first job at a clothing store at sixteen, I would spend my paycheck on makeup and clothes. I never worked to help my parents pay our bills.

My own connection to the land only known through play, gardening with my mother or in the mud pies I'd make for my dad that he'd happily pretend to eat.

Viktoria Valenzuela

Oh Say Can You See

By the dawn's early light, I think of skin; I think of how
Light can shine through my eyelids no matter how hard I close them.

I question, do they see
a lampshade at a neo-Nazi party?

When I think of eyelids
I pet mine with flower petals soaking.

We soak up the sun's rays to make chlorophyll.
Am I a daisy pushed up after someone has died?

When I think of flower petals
I think of honey bees hovering over the sex organs of flowers

and tongues
of black bears. Am I a black bear starving in the forest for lack of bees?

When I think of black bears
I think of polar bears who have white fur but black skin.

Am I a polar bear starving in the Arctic for lack of ice
and seal prey? When I think of I.C.E. I think of brown

skin, that looks just like mine, trying to make it in America.
Am I American if neo-Nazis' are running America?

When I think of America, my body aches
for something more protective than skin. Skin is only skin deep.

Skin is only skin
Deep. Black-Red-Yellow-Brown as brown can be.

Ayokunle Falomo

Sorry, Let Us Start at Birth, The Beginning

appears in *African, American*, winner of the New Delta Review Chapbook Contest, 2019

> They have a lottery. You pick people. Do you think the country is giving us their best people? No. What kind of a system is that? They come in by lottery. They give us their worst people, they put them in a bin, but in his hand, when he's picking them is, really, the worst of the worst. Congratulations, you're going to the United States. Okay. What a system — lottery system.
>
> ███████████████ on Dec 15, 2017
> while speaking to FBI academy graduates

If we should at all start,
let us at birth. Let there, of course,
be a certificate of birth. Let mine,
like anyone else's, be how I prove

that I was born. It is 2018
and would you look at that,
how there is no difference
at all between the calendar

of the year I was born
and this year's, if you
pay no mind to "the dates

for Easter and other
irregular holidays based
on a lunisolar calendar."

...

On the day
I was born
I was born
as another would
cease to be a son
his mother can name
as alive
if perhaps

the weight of this reality
that he was born
that she birthed him
hasn't already laid
claim of her breath

...

And the headline says:
**WALKER BECOMES
1ST EXECUTION IN 28 YEARS**

...

In 1990

I was born
the first

child & son
of my mother

which means

this year
I'll be 28 &

celebrating this
will be a reminder

that indeed
I was born.

...

And the news article says
he was the "first

inmate in Illinois to die
by lethal injection" & isn't

this too,
I think, a kind

of birth?

     ...

And again, the article says:
"At 12:01 a.m.,"

the buttons which the two
devoted disciples who'd been

assigned the role
of executioner pushed

delivered, to his condemned
body, the gospel, how
the end is near.

     ...

& of course, the trinity:

one drug for him to sleep,
the second for his breathing
to stop & the third, his heart

     ...

& of course
before this
the last
supper:
pan-fried
wild rabbit
gravy made
from the pan
drippings
biscuits
a dessert
of black

berry pie
with whip-
ped cream

...

& i cannot help but think how again i'm sorry we have to start at birth & how in order for a thing to become an answer if hunger were to be a question it has to be first born of its mother or of our Mother the Earth Yes let us start at birth & how if everything must have a genesis chapter one of this would speak of how on the 78th day from the day i was born a President's signature like my father & mother's on my birth certificate confirmed the birth of a thing & the thing is what will years from now grant my father & i entry into this country where as of today he whose name we refuse to name is still President & the one who was then said: "Today I am pleased to sign…the most comprehensive reform of our immigration laws in 66 years" & most days like today i still am not sure whether i am pleased by this or not but i know if it was not birthed there would be no form for my father to sign an agreement that we were both fine with leaving who knew my mother & sister & 3 brothers behind & that we were all fine with the reality that years after i would have left i will miss them so much that i will empty my ducts until there are no more tears left in them & that my father would empty his pores or purse same thing of his hard earned sweat up to the last drop & offer it as payment that'll grant them the opportunity to come join us but let us not speak of the years that will pass before this No No let us

...

It is 2014. And I am
no longer the boy I was (Amen)
when I left my mother but I am
still my mother's oldest son. Amen.

It is 2015 and my sister and brothers still are
and I am still their older brother. Amen.
And amen to the thick cord of blood, the bond
that time and distance won't break. Amen.

Tarfia Faizullah

Yr Not Exotic, but Once Ya Wanted to Be

appeared in *Poetry Magazine*, 2018

Whenever folks discuss finding themselves,
ya get kinda giggly. Maybe b/c ya found
yrself considering yr Armenian love
who preferred ya in both corset and bindi,
and it was for her ya begrudgingly waxed
yr jungle-scabbard ... Ya find yrself in the fret
of reclamation via musks all motherland-misty
(coconut milk, marine accord, mimosa tree). Last
weekend, ya found yrself in leggings to argue
again with yr Dominican love over the tender
texture of Texas tamales. Ya not-so-secretly want
to find yrself in a garden kissing a risk-
taking party until ya feel as good as a half-price
smoothie. Somehow, identity never finds ya
kohl-eyed in magenta blooms photographed
by a mixed-race admirer on a humid evening,
mostly b/c yr too busy galaxy-gazing
to be anyone's so-fair-and-lovely. Was that
a touch of pride or self-pity? Probably. But ya
just can't deal with another stranger's surprise
at yr love of both tequila and mango lassis.
Does yr Guyanese love truly expect ya to replace
the chicken & fish in yr diet with mushrooms
that arbitrarily? *You're so black*, yr told pretty
frequently. Ya don't know what to make of it:
humanity. Ever find yrself advised by
Bangladeshi Brooklynites? Like they know
yr bae Poetry! Loves, let's stop projecting
insecurities. But maybe it's like when ya tried
to be cheerful after a famous poet called ya Debbie
Downer for mentioning the hurricanes in yr other
sovereignty? Never don't find yrself coring

what music can be cleaved from a dull language
into an anomalous nationality. A personal theory:
we all behave oddly around fat titties. Now here
Poetry comes to say she wants to be an ode to what is
muddy. OK, baby. Here's to dank difficult borders,
gardens of ingrown perennials, fractured fins,
the wings of inner menageries. Here's to our own
empires of dirt — no one's pruned-perfumed colonies
of exotic beauty. This is not a poem! Or is it
an efficient exercise in surviving hysteria?

Texas Poets Speak Out 31

Poem Full of Worry Ending with My Birth

originally published in *Poem-a-Day* on April 10, 2018, the Academy of American Poets

I worry that my friends
will misunderstand my silence

as a lack of love, or interest, instead
of a tent city built for my own mind,

I worry I can no longer pretend
enough to get through another

year of pretending I know
that I understand time, though

I can see my own hands; sometimes,
I worry over how to dress in a world

where a white woman wearing
a scarf over her head is assumed

to be cold, whereas with my head
cloaked, I am an immediate symbol

of a war folks have been fighting
eons-deep before I was born, a meteor.

32 .... Contra

We Disdain

BLACK BIRTH; A PROTEST,
WE BORN WITH A DEATH SENTENCE
A STILL BORN, STILLBORN.
Omer Ahmed

Lacey Roop

Voter Registration

after Zoe Leonard

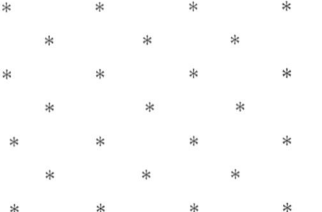

i want a people who will vote for school pencils over war missiles. i want a people who will always blame rape on the rapist & never the rape victim. i want a people who want to fund public education more than mass incarceration. i want a people who are more outraged over racism than they are by NFL players taking a knee. i want a people who regard journalism with the highest esteem instead of "news" outlets that use propaganda & pandering pundits. i want a people who can discern what is fact & what is an opinion; what is a truth & what is a deception. i want a people who believe in love & art & equality more than they do in hate & fear & division. i want a people who believe in science & climate change. i want a people who believe women have the right to choose what to do with their own bodies. i want a people who believe that human rights for all includes the poor & disenfranchised & the sick & the immigrant & the atheist & the gays & the trans, too. i want a people who hold law enforcement accountable & i want a people who hold elected officials accountable as well. i want a people who are more repulsed by the separation of children from their parents at the border & the poisoned water in Flint, Michigan & the wage gap between men & women & the disproportionate incarceration of black people & mass shootings & that over 32 million adults in this country are illiterate & that 1 in 4 Americans have to forgo health care because they can't afford it, than they are by same sex marriage & protests & having to wear a mask. i want a people who tell their sons it is okay to cry. i want a people who tell their daughters they can be the President. i want a people who show up every time the polls are open. i want a people who will always vote bigotry & xenophobia & racism & homophobia & sexism & greed & islamophobia & fear & hate & intolerance & indifference for the other— OUT.

Dear Male Members of the GOP

I had no idea you all were born with a vagina.
You make having one sound so easy.
The way y'all speak of them with such knowledge and confidence.
It sounds as if y'all have multiple vaginas
that you can just put on and take off whenever
you choose.

What a privilege it must be to have so much authority over
something you know nothing about.

What legacy we have as a nation
to have successfully set up institutions
that slice the throats of those
who need to speak the most.

For example—
when former Texas Governor Rick Perry was asked
how he knew so much about what women need he said,
Because I live with 4 of them— my wife, my daughter, and my 2 dogs.

If he was able to put his wife and daughter in the same category
as his bitches it is not a shock how he was so willing
to shut down necessary facilities needed
for the safety and treatment of women.

This issue isn't about baby killing.

That's something many states such as: Texas, Alabama,
Mississippi, Georgia, Arkansas, Louisiana,
Oklahoma, Indiana, South Carolina, etc…
all do once the baby comes out with all their education budget cuts
and making sure our prisons are filled with brown eyed and dark skinned
kids.

Y'all stand behind your actions by claiming you are here
to enact the will of God.
What soot must be in your souls congressmen to taint such pure a light.
I swear whatever god is behind you I will run the other way.

A woman's body is not a State's Right.

The floor of the Senate is not a place to be given a gynecological exam.
You don't know what kind of fear and shame can come with such a body
already. You wouldn't know what invasion of privacy it is to have your
cervix scraped.
If you listened to any of the testimonies in your jurisdictions
you'd know that a woman's body is not some sort of mechanical machine
that shuts down when she is raped.

We are not wind up dolls, gentleman.
You've let the jack out of the box and we ain't gettin' back in it.

Some people must wonder what your mothers must have done to you,
but I'd rather ask what kind of example your fathers must have set
to make you think that women are nothing
more but flies to be swatted at.
A woman's body is more important
than a political power struggle between two parties, congressmen.

People don't show up at abortion clinics
with ice cream cake and birthday candles.

Sometimes they come barely 13
with sunken shoulders and tear-stained cheeks
wanting a hand to hold and leave wishing there were instructions
on how to shed the fear, the guilt, the shame.

With so much talk about the sanctity of life
it is a wonder how the mother doesn't ever get mentioned
unless when she is being called a sinner or a whore.

This isn't about a woman's poor choice.
This is about women not being given the fundamental
right to make a choice at all.

We're not here to ask permission what we can do with our own bodies.
We're here to tell you that these bodies are not a weakness;
that these bodies have always been ours
and not some property that your government has ever
had the right to own.

ANEL I. FLORES

Breaking News: It's Not Okay

appears in *Latinx Subjectivities: A multi-genre anthology*, San Diego State Univ Press, 2020

>   *June 12, 2016*
>   *49 shot dead and 53 injured at gay nightclub, Pulse, in Orlando, FL*
>
>   *June 13th at 10:15 am*
>   *the next morning*

I called my mom because I longed for the feeling of being a baby, the feeling of being held, a space to safely crumble and cry. The ambulance lights still flashing my mind, their black and brown faces, look like all friends of mine.

And my mexican mami, who lovingly raised me on fresh frijoles, tortillas and peace-be-with-yous asked, "Mijita, Are you okay?"

I said "no," and wanted to tell her why. But she interrupted me before I could elaborate or spit out any feelings.

She told me, "We need to pray mija. The Virgencita, Jesucristo is waiting for us to give this mugre election up to them."

"No, but mami, I am scared about last night," and she continued, "I know, I know, that's why our Lord wants you to go to him."

I kept saying I am scared I am scared in my head. I wanted desperately for her to hear me, wanted her to just listen, like I wanted her to listen when I was scared twenty three years before, alone in my dorm, afraid because the student from Lubbock across the hall told me I was going to hell and her Odessa,Texas boyfriend smeared dog shit on my car. But Mami stopped talking to me back then, after she found out I was one of las otras, a lesbian.

I told her again, "Mami, I am scared of all the hate in the world right now," and she interrupted, "Mijita, I'm praying for our world, praying for the evil." And, I remembered when I was told by a praying man that I was evil for being a lesbian, a disgrace, disgusting, committing mortal sin. Then, I remembered that our soon to be president and his posse said those same words about me and all my queer and transgender hermanas y hermanos, my brown, black, muslim familia, my sisters, y mi gente coming to the US for dreams of quiet skies, food, and rest.

Then I remembered, my Mami is not the mean man I am afraid of.

She loves me, but somewhere in all the battles she had to fight, between being punished for speaking spanish, degraded by her white teachers, segregation, Vietnam, ovarian cancer, the Cold War, multiple sexual assaults from superiors, her lesbian daughter and the things she has packed away behind surviving the hits and blows, somewhere, she became so scared she stopped fighting. I reminded myself that my Mami has come a long way, gone through a lot, loves my wife, my daughters and me very much, so I tried again. "I am scared, Mami," I said, and "and our daughters are scared too. They're afraid, too." This time I thought my Mami would understand because she knows what it feels like to love her babies so much you'd kill for them, you'd live for them, you'd fight for them. She held my brother to her chest and promised to leave the country if he was called away to the Vietnam War. She felt the way I feel today, so I tried again. "Mami, I'm scared of Donald Trump and all the hateful people he's making more mad and more mean," I said. But something wouldn't let her hear me. Something wouldn't let the fear in and she interrupted again before I could continue.

"Mijita, we have to pray."

I wanted her to say she was going to come over, maybe make me caldo, sit with me, but she didn't. I wanted her to say she was ready to fight for me, but she didn't. The mucus broke up into my nose and I tried to tell her how scared I was again, but she kept praying and telling me it would be okay.

And, under my breath, on the other side of the phone I thought, But I am scared Mami. I was scared to hold Erika's hand at the grocery store, yesterday, Mami, just getting out of the car. And, I wanted to tell her that I let go of my wife's hand in the parking lot when a huge pick-up truck pulled up in front of us because I imagined someone jumping out to beat us with a two by four, like I had seen done before to a transgender woman on Main and Evergreen, on her knees. I wanted to cry and release my fears but she couldn't hear. She told me again, "Mija, it will be okay," and started to say goodbye. "Tell Erika and the girls I love them, mija," and I wanted her to stay on the phone so I could tell her why I was afraid to go to the bathroom alone. She told me it would be okay and to pray.

It is not okay.
It is not okay.
It is not okay.
I tried to say.
And, before I knew it
she wasn't on the other side of the phone
and I thought I was alone.
Then I found this pen
and this poem
and you were there
and I was here
and I began to tell you,
it is not okay.

It was not okay when the old white man told me and my wife, "Let me take you both home to feel what a real dick feels like."

It was not okay when the male coach told me at a pep rally he wanted to "rip the principal's red leather pants off and fuck her in the custodial closet."

It was not okay when my young, gay student was tormented by groups of boys near the library over and over until one day he never returned to school. Only to hear he died in the bathroom of causes we were never told, but a rope-burn around his neck.

It was not okay the day we realized there needed to be a suicide hotline just for lgbtq kids.

It was not okay when we realized we needed another hotline just for transgender kids becuase the suicide numbers were so high.

It was not okay when my wife's ex husband found it easy and foolproof to use our racist and homophobic laws to threaten her with the custody of our children and deportation.

It was not okay when a girl was being poked in her school hallway, and a football player told her she needed to send naked photos of her body to him, or else he'd do it again and again until he got what he wanted.

It was not okay when an adult man dragged my thirteen year old body to the beach, jammed his hand into my pants and my face into his. And it wasn't okay the three other times this same thing happened, at 6, 11 and 16.

It was not okay when our other daughter's roommate was raped in her dorm building by a swimmer at a Texas University and he got a slap on the hand. She dropped out of school because she was pregnant.

It was not okay when I held my father's gun to my head because I believed my fat, raped, ridiculed body was dirty and ugly, and my soul was not worthy of walking this world.

It is not okay that when you started reading this another woman was sexually assaulted in the US and since then, two more, and before you are done at least one more will be raped, grabbed, beat against their will or hit.

Is is not okay that forty nine of my queer black and brown sisters, brothers, fam and friends were gunned down dancing to disco cumbia and puerta negra on gay latin night just ours ago.

And this year 23 Transgender black and brown women will be murdered
next year 29
the year after that
we will lose 26 more black and brown transgender women to murder
In 2019 we will lose 27

In 2020
I'm losing count.
Guia espiritu Sylvia Rivera
spirit guide Marsha P. Johnson
sabia Gloria E. Anzaldua
wherever you are
doused in sparkles
love
and color
dance with us
dream with us
fight with us
free us
from this patriarchy.

Because
it is not okay

so do not tell me it is.
I am scared.
I am fueled.
I have a right to be.
I am not going to just pray.
I'm not going to let you leave here thinking it's okay.
I'm going to yell right back at the man who comes at me next time.
I am going to gather people together so we can take this patriarchy down ALIVE.
I am going to give my gente a safe place to thrive.
I am going to write our truths until someone listens.
I am going to walk you to your car so no one can lay a hand on you.
I am going to be a phone call away
when you want to tell me how scared you are
or you just want to talk about your scars.

This is not okay.
If you don't believe me, read this again.

Eddie Vega

Haikus

Taking kids from their
parents on the first day of
school is cold as ICE

Teaching methods have devolved
kids stress over lessons
in bullet points

We thought we were winning
the spades game
'til white people played the Trump card

Republicans welcome immigrants
to only one house
the White one

JOSHUA NGUYEN

I Tell My Aunt to Take Off The Stupid Red Hat

& she tells me:
that you & your siblings married
whitelooking people so shut up & eat
your bún bò huế
you ungrateful, son-of-a-generous
women who should be ashamed
to call you a son.
The only immigrants that I want
in this country are those who
almost starved
on a boat, fleeing
a war.
Finish
your food, or vomit
into the dog bowl & I'll
plastic-wrap it for you later.
Leave your bowl in the sink &
go kneel in front of the fireplace
with your forehead resting on the tips of the flames.
You are only good as the white wedge
that can prop white people
up. So, leave. Up
& away you go,
copying
black culture to the best
of your ability. Stand like your uncle
in front of the police scene & say nothing.
Protect your job, protect your image, but most importantly, protect
your pockets. Because in America,
you will never be looked
upon as American.
So, if everyone
is against
you
then might as well
choose the whitening side, I mean
winning side. Might as well use that model
minority to your liking. You like

bánh mì, right? You like
what French colonization
can taste like?
You like
bread
ripping the roof of your mouth?
Bite, chew, repeat until it bleeds the threads
of my red hat you despise so much. You can have
your morals, I'll collect the warm puddle
of you & place it in my phở
to sell at my restaurant
to the highest, white,
police officer.
I'll watch
them
choke on the broth,
kneel on the neck-bones they have lodged
in the back of their throats, & sell them
water to wash it down just so they
can stay alive & come
back the next day,
hungry,
 for—

Bill Moran

Saint Nikolas Challenges Senator Marco Rubio To A Fist Fight

+
PERCUTE PRO NOBIS
+

325 AD, Council of Nicea— a heretic priest denies the suffering of Christ. Saint Nikolas, enraged, marches onto the holy council floor, and knocks the priest out cold. Laid him out on the marble. Nikolas, patron of boxers, O.P.N.

2018 AD, Parkland, Florida— Senator Marco Rubio tweets bible verses for victims of the Douglas High School mass shooting.   And Saint Nikolas floats down from Heaven, to West Miami, to hold a press conference:

+

You tweeted Proverbs, "As dogs return to their vomit, so fools repeat their folly."

Do you know the next line? You should look up the next line.

"As dogs return to vomit–" Senator, I think you underestimate dogs.

"Humans dupe and are duped. A dog will give you an honest bark at the truth." Diogenes the Dog said that. A philosopher. With a boxer's name. He sniffed out liars like:

"dogs return to–" This vomit of yours, is it $3.3 million dollars from the NRA or your worthless prayers for #Parkland #Vegas #Houston # "We need more welders, less philosophers" you said.

Senator, have you worked with your hands? It is a highly philosophical act. I should know, Marco.

✢

If Christ comes back to Nazis in your state, this time he
will bleed from his knuckles. Believe.

Some philosophers talk with their hands. Some holy men
have a mean cross. The real St. Nick isn't real nice. Sorry.

But I do make house calls. I keep a list. I know heresy
when I see it.

✢

And I saw you, Senator, on TV,
tell a teen school shooting survivor,
to his face,
that you still won't refuse money from the NRA.
Dog to vomit.
I heard you

deny the least of these.

Heretic. Hypocrite. Lapdog.

✢

Boxer?
Oh, you're a Boxer huh?
Notice, Council,
that my opponent here thinks he can lay a hand on me
Like his hand's held anything. But money. And blood.
Like he really has fire arms
and South paws
and no gold-ringed hand up his back.
Ha. Don't reach, youngblood.

I see you
side-by-side with Pilate. Two Senators.
Washing soft hands
in bloody water.
In the second amendment.

Its author worshipped Voltaire, who said, "The Romans
built their greatest works of architecture for wild beasts to
fight in."

Senator, you built your coliseum in a high school in a
church where every week America holds mass
shootings. You gamble on dogfights between teens, but
you didn't build the walls high enough, Senator. The dogs
are in the stands. Clawing toward the box seats.

+

And I'm in your living room. I brought gifts.
A loose muzzle. Dog teeth. And Diogenes: "Other dogs
bite their enemies. I bite my friends to save them."

Amen, friend, you shall be saved.

For we share a god
the same way I share a name with the Parkland killer:
Nikolas. In his Slavic, "conqueror of the people". In my
Turkish, "victory of the people". Predator. Prayer. How do
you translate yourself?

+

I am Saint Nikolas, patron of boxers and students and
children.
I raised three children from the dead.
I dropped a priest in front of the Church.
I dropped gold down the chimneys of the poor.
I drop gold down your gun barrel,
old money out of office,
and the rich down my throat.
I drop to knee and pray with canine teeth.

+

How do you train?
Hit a bag?
Any fool can hit a bag.
Can you hit Truth?

A swarm of white phone lights
In the hands of teens?
Can you knock *that* light out?
A million teeth?
Eating up your donors online?
You every been eaten up?
Like God under the GOP?
Like vomit and dogs?
You know how much it hurts?
To watch a child die up close?
I have
heard the cries of America's teachers, parents, EMTs and
teens– Emma, David, the dead and alive, the badly bitten
and the still biting, amen, I plead your case to Heaven:

+

Hosanna,
hosanna,
we ask not for fire arms
but a boxer's hand,
saint's mouth,
honest bark,
and a hard truth:

Dogs eat their vomit. It's disgusting. But they clean up
their mess.

You find gun reform hard to swallow but, Marco, you
made this. It's disgusting. You have to clean it.

Or we will.
Wipe the floor with you.
In front of your cameras. Over Senate marble,
like the kids you drag over the second amendment
with a leash.
We'll get up and spit a little blood at the camera,
a signature on gun reform,
an outspoken knuckle across the NRA's gold teeth,
rinse and repeat,
until you are knocked loose.
Marco, the exit wound is always bigger than the entrance.

Every gunshot in Florida opens our giant mouth, again,
an exit wound chanting:

Nikolas!
Victory of the people!
We will win.
We are honest and barking,
holy dogs, holy saints,
with a holy
right
cross.

+
PERCUTE PRO NOBIS
+

O Sanctissima

+
ECCE DEBILES PERQUAM FLEBILES
+

Look, we are weak & deeply deplorable. Look, gingivitis in the mouth of the saint. Look, I grind my teeth like a hymn. O Sanctissima. O septicemia. O syrup for every breakfast. Blood on every toothbrush. Razor in every chocolate. trump in the white house. In Houston. "Thanks everybody, have a good time." With your uninsured mouth rot. Hometown under fucking water. The Gulf Coast is God's mouth and he rinses and rinses. Won't spit. We sit in it. Heaven's gutter. Ulcers in the cheek of Houston. Grime under grime on the altar. Upward we squint, thirsty. Even rats will chew their way into Heaven. We want your water, Lord. Your water.

+
ORA PRO NOBIS
+

Saint Apollonia, patron saint of dentistry, friend and advocate to those who fear the dentist– a rich man with gold hair and bleached teeth mocks your martyrdom. In the name of for-profit healthcare, of good business, he means to privatize and ransom back to us our bodies, which were fashioned in the image and likeness of a God he mocks.

I cannot afford his premium.
I cannot afford my teeth.

Blessed martyr–
an empire removed and ground down your teeth,

and then the the rest of you,
because you would not lie.

Apollonia, bless the teeth I lose in speaking truth,
and thank God for the ones I still have.

+
AUDI NOS
+

Apollonia, deliver us
from Senators and CEO's who would lie and do us harm,
who price gouge healthcare,
who let us go undiagnosed,
let us go voiceless,
let us die.
Let their teeth rot in their mouths.
Pull gold from their molars
and crown those of us who pay with jaw pain.
Our president wants pictures of dead presidents.
We don't want to hurt.

Apollonia, you who were tortured and killed by the State,
you refused anesthetic so that we wouldn't have to–
we ask for it now.

✢

TU MEDICINAM PORTAS DIVINAM

✢

You bring holy medicine,
Apollonia, who was taken from us like a baby tooth,
and grew back again in Heaven,
holy woman holding your own teeth.
Deign to appear to us in Houston,
gold molar on your necklace,
pincers in hand.
Be a root canal.
Rip the rich from us like soggy
drywall. Pull up the upper class like wet
carpet. Make new the mouth of the world.
Because the Gulf Coast is God's grin
and we are His teeth.
If we are broken, he cannot speak.
O, how we ache.
Apollonia, pray for Houston.
For gold grills over bleeding gums.
For gold crowns over cracked heads. For
He hath filled the hungry with good things;
and the rich He hath sent empty away.

✢
TOLLE LANGUORES
✢

Take away our languor, Apollonia. Your martyrdom demands that we be outraged at the cost of healthcare to the poor, to give thanks for the care we can afford, and to be courageous in seeking treatment. By your example, I find a dentist. And a therapist. I schedule an appointment. I fill the cavity of me. Thank you for these graces and more.

Apollonia, I grind my teeth in gratitude to you. Though I am weak and sinful, imperfectly I lift the rats of my heart up to heaven. I hold my yellow gums up to heaven. Holy shit, it hurts to open my mouth. Hurts worse to close it. With yellow gums I pray for us. With yellow gums I pray for Houston. With yellow gums I thank you for the health and healthcare I do have. With yellow gums I pray for those who don't. With yellow gums I say,

Amen, let our enemies know us by the yellow gums
that will eventually eat them,

Amen, yellow gums for ever
and ever,

Amen, this altar is awful
but it still works,

Amen, this altar is oily
but it can be cleaned.

I am weak and deeply deplorable.
But you bring holy medicine, amen.

Your water, Lord.
Your tasteless water.

Texas Poets Speak Out 53

+
AUDI NOS
+

+
ORA NOS
+

JOMAR VALENTIN

Declaration of Inconvenience

And just as we do the kings and queens of old,
future generations will study us in the history books;
or they will scroll past
whatever their generation considers a meme
the way some picket signs scurried out their shelters in place
back in the time when this chunk of America
removed their masks to reveal a new oath saying:
"We hold these truths to be self-evident,
that all are created equal…
endowed with certain unalienable Rights,
that among these are Life, Liberty…"
and the pursuit of a trim and a root touch up;
a margarita and a Corona.

A Declaration of Inconvenience,
against the mounting frustration of a cabin fever,
and a furlough on fuckery that no anti-vaxer would follow.
They flock to their governor's mansions chanting:
"Give me Liberty or give me death".
Despite being unoriginal,
is more of a summons of a self fulfilling prophecy
to which I say:
"Bitch, if you keep going outside you're about to get both!"
What a revolution they are having
that the urgency is so dire,
they couldn't be bothered to spell check.

Wow!
What a show of bravery
they will see in the next century,
when the then children will look at a book
like the now children look at a floppy disk
to download a memory file
to learn about the Great Karen Blockades
that littered the nation's streets;
blocking traffic into hospitals,
hurling insults are nurses and doctors

as if they were singing a re-written chorus to "No Scrubs" by Destiny's Child.
Look at Becky,
"hollering out the passenger's side of her best friend's ride"
because they haven't been to brunch in 2 weeks
and they just got their stimulus checks,
so 1200-dollar mimosas, please!
It will be an intoxicating story
when I tell my children, and my children's children
the true meaning of the word
viral.

How a bible story came to life in the year 2020
when these United States skipped to the 10th plague and sacrificed their first-borns;
made vulnerable the oldest of "We, the People",
arming them with nothing but a prescription of bleach and sunlight.
I can hear it now!
Their questions they will field.
So, when they ask me:
"Grandfather, but why didn't they just stay inside?"
I will say this:
"It's because this is America.
And we were told not to".
And just as we do the kings and queens of old,
the future generations
will turn their heads and eyes sideways
at the mistakes me made.

Omer Ahmed

America's Titties Only Produce Powdered Milk and Cobwebs

Or

America Pees on the Burning Bush at the Independence Day Block Party

Trump fingers the 4th of July,
and it dies from the Corona Virus.

There are no fireworks because,
because Zimmerman used up all the gunpowder on Trayvon.

Everyone in the Midwest dies of an overdose,
after ignoring the methamphetamines on their hot dogs.

No one dances,
because Miley Cyrus Stole all the black music.

California hears there might be a barbecue,
and cooks all of its residence so it doesn't show up empty handed.

Donald, Barrack, and George spill oil on the grills
despite literally everyone telling them not to.

The police show up and fire bullets
to replace the sounds of missing fireworks (and people).

The lights go out, because no one has paid the electric bill
so everyone is relieved when the klan shows up with torches.

Next year will be different.
Next year,
    there might be some vegan chili.

JOSHUA ROBBINS

American Augur

appeared in the Houston Chronicle

        We posted a large sign:
                KEEP OUT!,
    its letters red like animal blood.
And though we put many nails

      into it,
            you pulled it down.
Nothing we did
      could have kept you
               from us.

We burned
            candles in every corner
    of the house
Thinking you feared fire.

      We shouted, "We are sick with fever!"
But you sent a cold wind through our bodies.
    Our teeth
             fell from our skulls like seed.

In our fatigue
    nothing grows.
             Months have passed.
Now we argue

      about when
            you will finish us off.
Even in our dreams
    we wonder.
           Some nights,

We can hear the bed
    muttering plans for escape.
Closet doors
      no longer open.

If we cut off our ears
And offered them
    or scraped out our tongues

And made a paste
           to smear
   across our foreheads,
Would you then
         pass by our door?

    Though we have heard it has happened
This way
    for centuries,
  we are not comforted.

There is nothing
   you cannot take
Away from us.

Passing Paradise

appeared in *Praise Nothing*, Univ. of Arkansas Press, 2013

    Like a man blindfolded and asked to kneel
    who cannot hear the bolt strike the cartridge
    after it enters the chamber, its click
    like classroom chalk breaking on black
    slate, a sound small but definite:
                                  one stone
    kicked up against the curb, a pocketknife
    shut, a finger snapped. So, what then
    of the old Romanian sweeping strip-mall
    theater's sidewalk, for whom heaven
    has become nothing
                         but an age-dulled
    marquee gone unlit for years,
    its one *Paradiso* meant to entrance
    whomever drives past and happens
    to look up? I saw a film once in which
    a wealthy man moved
                            all he owned
    into his parlor. Each morning, he fired
    two rounds into the pile and, finding it
    all still there, returned to sleep
    beneath a thin blanket on the lacquered hardwood
    of his indoor bowling lane.
                            It's not easy
    to remember when we first began
    to loathe irony. South of Bucharest and beside
    the ditch banks and bare hills, the soaked
    fields' sheen, where no one is asking if History
    is yet up off its knees,
                          powerful men
    have reproduced TV's *Dallas* ranch. Weekend
    getaways for sale. Even Larry Hagman's
    been there. When he arrives, the executioner
    carries the rifle indifferently,
    swings it like a broom.

Vincent Cooper

Lyft Ride

"Tomorrow who's gonna fuss?" – The Replacements

The middle-aged Army veteran says:
    I got no problems with trans in the military
    but in the moment of truth
    they just won't shoot.
    They're only here for a college degree...
    Can't trust them to protect our country,
    because their core isn't to kill.
    On the battlefield, with pants soaked in piss...
    Talkin' about a college degree...
    In the Army, we have crackheads asking to delay their urinalysis.

                                Recalibrate your code [Primogeniture]
        Your grandfathers   roaming guilty   in the ghost world
                                                                              can't hurt you
              or keep you   in the closet   anymore.
                                Recalibrate your code [Primogeniture]
                                                  Do BIPOC this favor
                    We want to see our non-binary grandchildren grow.

Edward Vidaurre

Men, Women, and Children

autumn
        means nothing when your hands are wrapped around
iron bars
        but a poet in prison writes the seasons into existence for his
cell mates
        who become squirrels, trees, orange & brown leaves.

politicians
        will always be turkeys, in any season.
prayers
        are contrails against the vast expanse in the heavens, unheard

autumn
        brings us closer to the season of death, the season of birth, of
anxiety
        that triggers a finger lickin' trigger happy wide eyed war on the
minority.

Men
        Are not safe on our streets, much less in prison.
Women
        Are raped and killed and mistreated in all systems & all borders
Children
        Told to do well in school and be future leaders in our society.

How do you suppose they do that when their families are torn apart?

I Believe

after Blas De Otero

I believe in the human being. I have seen
children torn away from families, daughters
swaying from closets and ceilings, men face down
on gutters with blood trickling into sewers,
and I believe it.

I believe in peace. I have seen stars
shoot from one end of the sky to the other
side of heaven, planets go dark, and ashes
come down like rain, I have seen and I believe it.

I believe in you, my country. I will tell you
what I have seen: I have seen rivers run dry
with footprints the size of wallets and knives
with crimson songs, playgrounds with echoes
of children's laughter and rain that taste like
border tears; still my heart beats for more; I have seen it
and I believe it.

Let's End This Nightmare

I
Summer heat, tear gas
Burns the eyes to silence words
Portland goddamn you

II
on the floor
we counted the broken glass

Then we counted the minutes
Then we counted the bodies

Then we counted last breaths

III
Breonna Taylor

Slept,

Her dreams exited through six doors.

President Trump

Had four years,

Slept through them all

End this nightmare.

Joaquín Zihuatanejo

Poetry Prompts for Detained Children

Write about the untouchable. Something out of arm's reach, like god, the stars, or you.

Write an ode to misfits. A poem of praise for those who don't belong here or there. A lyric ballad for the children of nowhere. Employ the interjection *Oh* at some point in the poem. Remember it can be used to capture their joy or your pain.

Write a *how to* poem about something mundane that most people take for granted. How to hear your mother's voice. How to see the sky. How to trust a man in a uniform. How to breathe.

Write about things that are out of order. Broken vending machines. Raging defense attorneys. This border. This country.

Become that something that doesn't love a wall. Give it a name. A history. Tell us in verse why it hates walls so desperately. Why we all should.

Write a poem from the point of view of a firefly trapped in a jar with holes hammered into the lid. Make the reader experience what it is to be something tiny and beautiful locked away into a restrictive space.

Write a persona poem in the voice of something that doesn't acknowledge the existence of borders: monarch butterflies, FM radio waves, rivers.

Write a sestina where the six repeating words are:

mother
tongue
light
slip
silt
forgive

Write a poem about a young person armed not with a fist or a gun, but an idea. An idea that could free us all.

Write a poem about a door unlocking. Opening. And what it feels like to walk through it without anyone there to tell you, *you can't.*

Octavio Quintanilla

These works first appeared in *derlands*. Source for altered texts is Gloria Anzaldúa's *Borderlands / La Frontera: The New Mestiza*, 4th edition.

Poder

Texas Poets Speak Out 67

<u>Under my fingers</u>

the iron <u>sky</u>
Mexican chi<u>ldren</u>

<u>press my hand</u>
crowned w<u>ith</u>

<u>flatlands</u>
the <u>Magic Valley of South Texas</u>

The Graves

After Mexican-Am███████████ed a train in Brownsville, ███████████ began lynchi███ Texas Rangers ██████ the brush an██████ ██████ lynched ████us a matter of months, ████████ to Mexico, leaving their █████████ Anglos afraid that the *mexicanos* would seek U.S., brought in 20,000 arm███ ps to put an end to the social protest movement in Sou███ ██as. Race hatred had finally fomented into an all out wa███

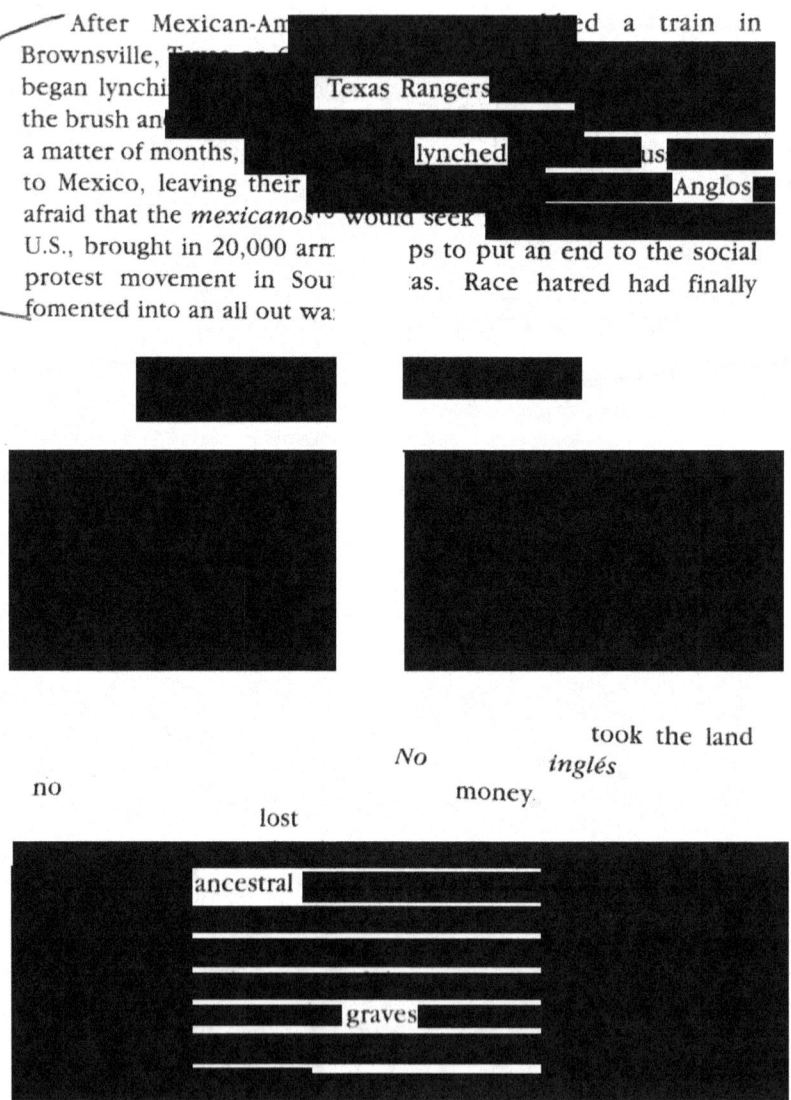

took the land
No
inglés
no money.
lost

ancestral

graves

DANNY STRACK

Human Rights

You have the right to remain silent.

You also have the right to an attorney.
You might think you have the right to a phone call,
but that depends on what state you're in.

And your attorney might be assigned by the court,
which they don't have to do till you've been indicted,
which means you might be sitting in jail for half a year.

But you do have the right to remain silent during that time.

Rights are weird like that.
A lot of "maybes" and "mights."
They say you have the right to an attorney,
but they don't tell you your attorney might have more cases than the best could handle,
and they might not be the best.
And you can't switch if you aren't satisfied.

You have the right
to be arbitrarily assigned the cheapest attorney the state could find.
But that's alright - a good number of them might be tireless public servants
working hard to make a difference,
maybe you'll get one of those.

When the Declaration of Independence states
that we are all endowed with the inalienable rights to
life, liberty and the pursuit of happiness,
it's nothing but a bold and lofty lie,
never enshrined as law.

When a thing is "inalienable," it can't be taken away.
But a cop can take your liberty and prison can keep it.

A cop might even take your life like it meant nothing,
and get away with it.

And even if a good cop read you your rights,
a jury or judge might still give you the death penalty.
And it's pretty hard to pursue happiness when you're dead.

These things we call "rights" are just agreements we make about how we want things to be.

But the Bill of Rights is basically a list of things you can do to lose
your job or your life:
practice the wrong religion, say the wrong thing, bare arms
in the wrong place,
be the wrong kind of person...

Right now we're fighting to make healthcare a human right,
and that sounds amazing, incredible, awesome.

But while we're arguing about it,
We might remember that nowhere in the constitution does it stipulate
that we have the rights to even the most basic things we need to live.

You don't have the right to fresh water or clean air,
just ask anywhere with lead in the pipes with no plans to replace,
just ask everywhere in America where breathing is a choke right now.

You don't have the right to shelter,
just ask the half million homeless making their homes under
highway overpasses
in every city from sea to shining sea.

We might remember the two and a half million in prison --
More people than live in Houston, the largest city in Texas,
many not only denied liberty,
but forced to work for pennies in for-profit industries,
we might call it modern slavery.

We might remember that every day,
the people with power are working to erode the limited rights the rest of us
have left.

But you don't have to fight back,
you don't have to speak up.

Texas Poets Speak Out 71

Even if they kill you,
that's the one thing they can't take away:

Your right to remain...

The Best Way to Make People Believe Anything Is to Repeat It

The Best Way to Make People Believe Anything Is to Repeat It

The Best Way to Make People Believe Anything Is to Repeat It

The best way to make people believe anything is to repeat it.
Over and over again.

Now you might not believe me when I tell you
the best way to make people believe anything is to repeat it.
But I know I can convince you because
the best way to make people believe anything is to repeat it.

And you might say, "hang on a second --
I think the best way to get people to believe me is strong arguments and evidence that I'm right."
And you might be a Democrat,
still convinced that science is real,
and things are more complicated than they seem,
when I know in my gut that
the best way to make people believe anything is to repeat it,
and you aren't going to be able to convince me otherwise.

You might convince some people with strong arguments and evidence --
other people within your liberal bubble --
but I don't have to convince everybody that
the best way to make people believe anything is to repeat it,
I only have to convince enough people to cloud the issue and *confuse you.*
And fact is, most people don't have the time or energy to research whether or not it's true that
the best way to make people believe anything is to repeat it.
So I can get away with saying that
the best way to make people believe anything is to repeat it,
and you're going to have a hell of a time proving me wrong!

You're going to go around telling everyone,
"This guy, Danny Strack,
he says that, '**the best way to make people believe anything is to repeat it,**'
which is obvious bullshit."
And a lot of people will agree with you.
But some other members of your audience might perk up their ears and say to themselves,
"Hmmm... maybe this Danny Strack guy is onto something, maaaybe
the best way to make people believe anything is to repeat it."

And so, in the process of trying to refute me,
you're just spreading my name and message further than I could have without your help!

So I'm sticking to my talking points.
The best way to make people believe anything is to repeat it.
I didn't come on this news program to have a real conversation,
I'm here to sell you on the idea that
the best way to make people believe anything is to repeat it.

You might have asked me about COVID or obstruction of justice,
or the president's ties to Russia,
but all I'm going to tell you is that
the best way to make people believe anything is to repeat it.

You might have asked me about propaganda,
or hypnosis,
but all I'm going to tell you is that
if you repeat anything enough times,
with enough authority,
if enough people are standing next to you saying the same thing,
then everyone will start to doubt everything!

The best way to MAKE people BELIEVE anything is to repeat it.

Do you even know the difference between propaganda and hypnosis?

Do you even know that **the best way to make people believe anything is to repeat it?**

Do you even know the difference between hypnosis and being lulled into a false sense of insecurity?

Do you even know the difference between propaganda and being lulled... to sleep?

Texas Poets Speak Out 75

We Riot

ALL LIVES MATTER AND
MAKE AMERICA GREAT AGAIN -
TWO MORE WHITE LIES
Eddie Vega

Sip

Declare Independence

Riots have always kept this country together
Our independence doctrine confirms what we're willing to do
Due to a country no longer guaranteeing civil rights
Riot
Burn it
War
Repeat until independence is found
July 9th 1776
Statue of King George III torn down
The oppressor
Mimicked again July 2020
Statue of Stonewall Jackson torn down
The oppressor
White people mad again
Trying to redeem their streak
Forgetting we're at the top of the repetition
Our civil rights violated again
Riot
We have a civic duty to defend these rights
Burn it
Finding ourselves having to reexplain our rights and relationship to government
War
Guess they don't see the resemblance
Don't recognize their own rules
Guess black and brown is only a token
A casualty
Make it seem everything be just fine if we was gone
A land colonized
Ironically writes that it wants to be seen as an asylum for those persecuted
No one is protected on this soil
Just words written on paper
Acting as a clock reset
Riot
Burn it
War
Independence is never found on land designed for oppression

NAOMI SHIHAB NYE

Propriety (take two)

How dare   they   they   they

say   say   say

anything we can or cannot do with our own

red and blue

We will wear our masks

to honor you

We are voting for ourselves

unbound by convention

con man convention

righteous posturing

all the ways to say

money

hold oneself above

be better than

someone else at the corner

We are voting for the four year old

eating a tangerine

if we please

sitting on sand under a canopy in the rain

78.. Contra

even he knows

telling the truth is preferable

let's not spend our succulent old age

hating people

be hopeful again

EXIT doors of hotel stairways

swizzle sticks of memory spinning me

through so much dullness

red and blue

M.R. "Chibbi" Orduña

The United Corporations of America

first printed in *OTRO/PATRIA*, 2019

the US Constitution was written in 1787 and starts like this:

> "We the People of the United States, in Order to form a more perfect Union, establish Justice, insure domestic Tranquility, provide for the common defense, promote the general Welfare, and secure the Blessings of Liberty to ourselves and our Posterity, do ordained establish this Constitution for the United States of America."

a bold proclamation
    a promise of a better tomorrow
a sales pitch to the skeptical?
    do these words still ring true?
if the US Constitution was written today,
    I think it would sound more like this:

"We the People have been diminished to include only the Elected, the accomplished to Power, powering over its Citizens, molding these United States, in Order to form a more perfect Profit, establish Justice that just is biased by nature. Naturally, we must ensure Domestic Obedience, ensuring Dependence on this system, tranquilizing Transgressors. We provide Defense against the Common People, and for the Companies that form our great Nation, promoting, generally, everyone, above a certain Tax Bracket, and abolish any Welfare that compromises the Security of our Assets. We will continue to bless Ourselves, and our Prosperity, ordaining this Constitution
For these United Corporations of America."

America lost its soul
to the highest bidder / left its citizens
at the base of the auction block / it happened
little by little, then all at once
while we were all watching
Big Money put Washington in its little pocket

and we   were sort of fine with that   so long as
they didn't take away My MTV   or BET

traded in Real Change
for Real Housewives // News for Entertainment // Dissent for Distraction
how could we care when we can't even C-SPAN
what's in it for me?

lost sight of the Big Picture when we swallowed that Capitalist Pill

cuz I was born to flex
    diamonds on my neck
nothing in this world
    that I like more than checks![1]

                                                    right?

Bad Bitches   don't wear red bottoms and make money moves
Bad Bitches   wear suits and make deals
behind closed doors – that line their pockets –
make lines at food pantries – unemployment offices –
no high-speed races just
                    \\racial divides\\
maybe Shonda Rhymes should write for CNN
then maybe we could see an end to this

                         Washington DC's basically a lifetime of *Scandal*
                         everyone knows *How to Get Away with Murder*
They don't pull triggers
              they pull funding and a nation suffers

             Government shuts down – People go unpaid –
             Aid gets delayed – as a majority of Americans
             continue to slave away – at a job they hate – as
             the Rich get paid – and the rest of US get debt:
                 do I have your attention yet?
                 are you not entertained?
                  'cuz this show gets
                   renewed for
                    another
                     season
                      every
                       four
                       years

---

[1] "Money" by Cardi B, Kelnord Raphael, Anthony White, Jorden Thorpe, Pardison Fontaine

Butti-Ho, or Where Would You Rather be Sitting, in the Oval Office or on Your Husband's Face

After the woman in Iowa who wanted to change her vote when she found out that Pete Buttigieg is a homosexual

Anticipation is the slogan
       of any seasoned bottom
Can't be full of shit
       before you get fucked

To take on a big dick you gotta plan ahead
And that midwestern Caucus was thick

       We know
With great anal
       comes great responsibility

       Pete

I thought you running meant
       we didn't have to be scared anymore
I am terrified America
Comfortable with the Ken-doll version of gay marriage
Talks of trade   your balls
           their votes
Don't use that educated tongue of yours
       To kiss their puckered ass
         Eat your husband's
       Pete

You acted like the fact that you suck cock shouldn't matter

       But it does

    it does it does it does it does it does it does it does
    it does it does it does it does it does it does it does
    it does it does it does it does it does it does it does
    it does it does it does it does it does it does it does
    it does it does it does it does it does it does it does
    it does it does it does it does it does it does it does

To every fluid boy that couldn't walk a straight line | the eyeliner turned black eye | nail polish chipped off before coming home | for those of us that couldn't come home | for the girls who were actually boys | the boys that were actually neither

Pete

Can't shift focus to the issues
When the issue is today in America

you can be gay

but not too gay

Is that why your policies were so moderate?
Your lifestyle too extreme to be electable?
Lean too far left you might surprise into a pride parade?

Pete

Using politics as a ball gag does not make you kinky
Mr. Poster-boy   Mr. Pride Marshal
Front Page -> Model Citizen -> Clean Cut -> Castrated
                                Easy to swallow
Wanted to be Commander-in-Chief; couldn't be seen as submissive in bed

Pete

If there's one thing college taught me
You can be a bottom and still be on top

Chins clean, held high
Wrists limp, an unbent spine
Hips cocked and a tongue pop
How you think we've survived thus far?

Pete

From Stonewall to   Regan   to   Westboro   Baptist   Church
It was never the people that chose to lead   that fought
It was those that were forced to fight   that lead

And you couldn't pick up the proverbial brick
For the snowball's chance of being palpable
Straight passing is a privilege
You thought you could ride past the primaries

Texas Poets Speak Out.. 83

Trying to Milk a cookie cutter campaign
                                      no one is gagging on vanilla

So sit back in South Bend
This country isn't done fucking us
                            over

Amalia Ortiz

Power in a Woman

appears in *The Canción Cannibal* Cabaret, Aztlan Libre Press, 2019

> *after "There is Power in a Union" by Billy Bragg,*
> *after "There is Power in the Blood" by Lewis Jones,*
> *and after "Battle Cry of Freedom" by George F. Root*

There is power in the family, power in the home—
Power in the hands of the mother—
But we're stronger with our sisters than when we each stand alone.
There is power in a woman.

All the wars of our oppressors demand innocent blood.
The mistakes of the machos, we must pay for.
From the cities and the ranchos to colonia roads of mud,
daughters divided are conquered in each man's war.

¡Mujeres unidas defending our rights!
Down with machismo! All women unite!
With our families and our allies, we will form a righteous clan!
There is power in a woman!

Now, I'm longing for the day when we are decolonized.
Brutality and injustice can't defeat us.
But to defend ourselves, my sisters, we must be organized,
when the patriarchy exploits and mistreats us.

¡Mujeres rebeldes luchando por la paz!
For every mother, we rise with our cause!
For the orphan, for the widow lasting peace will soon be won.
There is power in a woman!

¡Mujeres unidas defending our rights!
Down with machismo! All women unite!
With our families and our allies, we will form a righteous clan!
There is power in a woman!

Texas Poets Speak Out... 85

Demolish

appears in *The Canción Cannibal* Cabaret, Aztlan Libre Press, 2019

after Demolición by Los Saicos

Ratatatatatatata! Yeah! Yeah! Yeah! Yeah!

Unite to destroy the oppressive state.
Unite to destroy the oppressive state.
Unite to destroy the oppressive state.
Unite to destroy the oppressive state.

Tear it down. Tear it down.   Tear it down. Tear it down.
Unite to destroy the oppressive state.
Tear it down.   Tear down the oppressive state.
Tear it down.   Tear down the oppressive state.

Ratatatatatatata! Yeah! Yeah! Yeah! Yeah!

We must overthrow the oppressive state.
Overthrow! Overthrow!   Overthrow! Overthrow!
We must overthrow the oppressive state.
Overthrow! Overthrow!   Overthrow! Overthrow!

Yeah! Yeah! Yeah! Yeah!   Yeah! Yeah! Yeah!
Yeah! Yeah! Yeah! Yeah!   Yeah! Yeah! Yeah!
Yeah! Yeah! Yeah! Yeah!   Yeah! Yeah! Yeah!
Yeah! Yeah! Yeah! Yeah!   Yeah! Yeah! Yeah!

Tear it down. Tear it down.
Tear it down. Tear it down.
Tear it down. Tear it down.
Tear it down.

Ratatatatatatata! Yeah! Yeah! Yeah! Yeah!

RODNEY GOMEZ

Notes on the Infection

You say no one can argue
with the fact that we suffer
an immigration problem in this country.

When you speak I hear a jar
crack open on teak
exposing its marmalade.

No one comes to clean it up
except a thrush
who runs her sticky beak
through rind
like a surgeon.

<<>>

You think *animals*.
I know this because you've hidden
a camouflaged feeder in a lease,
a tin man to deer whose axe an acre away
cuts bone from body.

You'll think death was deserved.
But you are the interloper here.

<<>>

In Nogales a man is arrested for pouring
water into barrels for refugees.
It isn't spring but it saves.

Whenever you cite the law I hear
that even the rumor of infection
spreads infection.

I hear that if a sick child sleeps
in your house
you burn

the whole house down
with whatever she touched.

C.L. "Rooster" Martinez

My Angry Song

(for Woodie Guthrie & 2020)

This land is your land
This land is my land

now run this football   100   200   400 yards   give up
your body give US your ghost   give your sanity to explosions
and doors shut too hard
give up your children for boxes and flags
we'll give them a day
(well, it's not really *their* day   it's actually a day for all names in
Arlington and dead numbers in textbooks   stats   *can't make an*
omelet without a few touchdowns) let us   impart rage into your
once   graceful steps   good boys   deserve
trembling hands   mass death   in this country
never warrants a reset   a t-shirt at best   riot if you want
real attention
kneel and be spat on

they say this land was made for you and for me
but where is the evidence?
a *Chili's* in ruins will spark a race war   faster than a dead bullet finds
a black child
or thousands of Mexican children   missing
we'll give you an American Dream   but
keep it in your head
                                                         in a sense
you being here   means you're living proof
don't you feel it?
when you eat at McDonald's?
listening to commercials selling anti-streak deodorant? don't you feel it?
when the redwoods cinder and the gulf stream is rank?
do you?
and what if, it was?   a myth or dream allowed before sleep?
         is that heaven?
who installed the floors   and the A/C?   who painted this joker?   do they
get to live here   or is there another loophole to fall into?

This land was made for you and me

If a Latino calls you a Coconut that means you're brown on the outside, white on the inside; a Loconut is a pejorative—I made up— that means you're brown on the outside, Donald Trump on the inside.

there is a hell on earth for people without people
for children sprouting roots
on the wrong side of the frontlines
on the erasers edge
on the spear tip and the canines of war dogs

the god of irony taught many lessons—

taught: protecting murdered generations
meant teaching children to be muted ghosts

taught: the people of the sun to quit reaching for the sky

taught: "being American" is "acting respectable"
                                      means: remain alive

taught: treat tongues as welcome mats
say shit like: *I'm not Mexican / I'm Spanish*
(knowing their damn abuelas
crossed the same fronteras
as our abuelas)

taught: when faced with a bullet
pretend to be a gun too

Loconuts por favor
stop changing your names from *Esperanza* to "Hope"
your last name says: *Si se Puede!*
your actions say: Build that Wall!

90 .... Contra

acting dead for survival
<shred in the beaks of two eagles>
you sought more worlds to die in

thought: *they kill heroes / have none*
bury your hands cotton / disappear into boll
be not made of the morning and the dying dusk
be not made of brighter things than what we were taught we weren't.

Kevin Burke

A Sincere Toast

appears in *Going Down Swinging*, Timber Mouse Publishing, 2019

So, money, right?
So long as people are making it we're good, right?
So long as the people in charge are making it, we all win, right?
Because it trickles down, right?
Like a pyramid of champagne glasses, right?
It must be,
it must be like that because you drink champagne when you celebrate, right?!
And we're all gonna get rich so let's celebrate, right!?
I mean, it's not like there's any incentive for the glass at the top to make itself bigger, right?
Like one gigantic champagne glass?
Like a kiddie pool on a stem, right?
Like it keeps getting bigger and bigger and no champagne
comes down to the smaller
champagne glasses that make up the vast majority of the pyramid, right?
No.
That would be ridiculous.
Why would the big champagne glass do that?
Then the rest of us couldn't celebrate all the money we're gonna make, right?
'Cause we've been told we're gonna get that champagne.
Never mind that the weight of a gigantic champagne glass
full of champagne at the top
would put so much pressure
on the other champagne glasses that we couldn't even
move out of the pyramid if we wanted to, right?
'Cause we're gonna get some of that champagne, right?!
It's not like that big glass on top can get any bigger, right?!
Because even if it does, we'll just get more champagne, right?
Because this whole set up
this whole pyramid
is the only way we're all gonna get some champagne, right?
That's what the folks with the big glass at the top say
and they gotta know
look at that glass!
It's so big!

So let's open more champagne!
Here!
This one's huge!
Vintage oil champagne!
There's so much fucking champagne!
Who cares if we get too drunk and drill too many holes
in our liver, right!?
Forget those smaller bottles!
There's no way the sun or wind could ever make
this much fracking
I mean fucking
champagne!
Why even bother, right!?
Or how about this one?!
Pop the precision guided cork off
that bottle of military champagne!
Look at all the champagne!
Blood might be thicker than water
but you can drink away the stains
with champagne!!!
We should buy more of these
bottles, right!?
Look at how much champagne is
in that big glass
at the top now!
There's so much
we're all getting
some now, right?!
Those glasses on the bottom
that are still empty
they're just not trying
hard enough, right?!
They're just lazy
or made of glass
or plastic
or something with
less integrity.
Whatever it is
it's different and scary.
Not like the crystal glass
at the top!
Why can't they just be like

the glass at the top?!
That's what we're
all trying to do, right?!
We've just gotta
make ourselves
out of crystal!
Right!
Any other way
of doing things
would be a
terrifying idea!
That big glass
at the top is
afraid of any
other idea
and they have
such a big glass
of so much
champagne
that they
must be right
right?!
So there's
nothing wrong with
being scared
and killing
or locking up
anyone
who disagrees
right!?
Right!
And we should
celebrate
getting rid
of those
scary scary
different
small
glasses!
Unscrew
this bottle of
prison

industrial
champagne!
There
it is!
The more
we're afraid
and the more
we put
behind
bars
and the
more
we build
to kill
and spill
the more
champagne
there
is
right?!
Right!
So
cel
eb
erate!
Dri
nk
up!
We'
re
go
nna
be
rich!
We'
re
go
nna
be
rich!

Texas Poets Speak Out... 95

Ev
ery

on

e

of

u

s

r

i

c

h

Yankee Devil in God's Country

appears in *This is Ramshackle Freedom*, Timber Mouse Publishing, 2017

And they say I just don't get it.
That I'm a *yankee devil*
in god's country
who likes hitting below the bible belt.
That *he don't get*
good southern humor.
That a boy from Chicago
don't belong here.
Or in white house for that matter.
That there must be something wrong
when I don't laugh as a *good southern comic*
who's probably never listened
to a full hip hop album
reduces the art form
to a violent racist caricature
conveniently forgetting
that god loving Johnny Cash said
I took a shot of cocaine and I shot my woman down.
That I must be crazy
when I don't agree that
Donald Trump *tells is like it is.*
That I don't understand the south.
That I don't understand their south.
That I don't understand
how ignorance and simplicity
are held as virtues
and how people
fearfully load their John Waynes
in the face of tomorrow
wishing for dixie
then cocking their dicks and whistling.

This is not the south that got me to stay
This is not the welcoming arms of strangers who have become my family.
This is not my south.
My south's sweet tea won't rot out
the frost bite of my teeth.
My south won't let my birth city's big shoulders shut the fuck up.

I will use their strength to hold up
what I know to be true about my south.

My south's city of powdered sugar and voodoo
was gargled and spit out by the ocean
then got back up
and still blew it's brass brightly.

My south's communities lock arms and hearts
and dig in against overwhelming geography and time.

I moved to a place where
after all this time
people still resist
persist
and pull down flags from capitols
in the face of centuries of state backed bigotry.

(Head-check:

Even if the confederate flag is just about heritage, the swastika was a tibetan symbol for good luck, but some racist assholes went and ruined that for the world too. Tough shit. Get over it. Quit acting like overdue fair treatment is oppressing you when you've been sitting in a privileged booster seat you children.)

What do I know about the south?
I know art here is more than art.
It's fucking necessary for survival
and its beauty is like its flowers
brilliant, thorned, and drought hardened
for survival.

I know that the word *y'all*
is efficient, y'all.

I know the food here will make you a believer.
Praise be to smoked meats.
Praise be to anything involving tortillas.
In the name of biscuits, gravy,
and the holy grits,
Hallelujah!

Motherfucker,
you were born here.
I came here by choice.

Don't tell me that I don't understand
what I've come to love.
Don't tell me I don't understand
the place I call home
or the people I call family.

There is a warmth here that sticks
long after the sun goes down.
I've come to recognize it
in the summer strung christmas lights
in my friend's eyes.
I've learned to wear it well.

I've got a straw hat for the sun now
and won two belt buckles down here.

This is the south I live in.
I'd love to see you try to
come and take it.

Ebony Stewart

Compassion Fatigue

appears in *Home.Girl.Hood.*, TimberMouse Publishing & Write About Now Publishing, 2018

To the white womxn whose YouTube comment said,
she is tired of every other American poem being about race or rape.
I'm not sure if compassion fatigue happens
because no one taught you how not to be oppressed
or because no one taught you how not to be the oppressor,
but your comment reminds us that *no one cares about us but us.*[2]
You're right. There are no new topics,
just old problems written into new pleas
to a country that refuses to reckon with its own sickness.
We Americans,
land of the free,
can only keep our motto
if we keep our mouths closed.
And isn't that what all rapists want?
Control and a silenced victim.
Do you realize someone has stopped listening to this poem
because I am first black and also a womxn?
Black, if I'm alive still.
Womxn, if I haven't disappeared yet.
Got anything anybody in the world might need
except my voice—
which means,
my body must be what's left for the taking.
I'm not sure how we became *treasures we can't afford to keep.*
But there are womyn of all kinds who've been raped;
who also hoped their warm bodies' heart would stop beating,
but still went to work the next day.
What we know is,
it's hard to comfort a girl who doesn't let on she's hurting.
So praise every womxn who speaks out against her rapist in an effort to heal.
Praise the ones who didn't,
but got their healing from the poems you are tired of hearing.
How easy it must be to only sit through the happy.

---

[2] "Liliane" by Ntozake Shange

While we try an' believe the only thing we need to remember about
suffering is that,
eventually,
it ends.
Three times now, on social media, I've watched a black person be murdered
because the United States is still making us pay for the way we look or the
guilt it feels.
But a person of color's only glory hallelujah is
as long as we didn't die, then we didn't die.
Do you realize
that when our mothers say, "I love you,"
she is also saying,
stay alive,
come back to me whole, in one piece,
and not a hashtag
or another dead *nigga* whose death she'll have to watch on repeat?
Us poets,
whose duty is to write about the times,
write, because we don't know when we'll become extinct.
We are what's left.
Black ink from black poets, who dare to respond to all this black death,
instead of hiding behind everything we're thinking.
How privileged your life must be,
that you can be tired of hearing poems about race or rape,
while we write about an extinguished race
and violated bodies that keep being raped.

It's not hard to believe you're tired,
but can you empathize with how exhausted
we
must
be?

We Dream

Wanna save the world?
Be a hero? Fight evil?
Defeat fascists? Vote.

Glori B

Natalia Treviño

Sorrow #2. The flight into Egypt

"Arise and take the child and His mother and fly into Egypt . . .
For it will come to pass that Herod will seek the child to destroy Him"

for it came to pass that his life was a threat to power and that he would be destroyed, for it came to pass that their lives were a threat to power and that their lives also destroyed for it came to pass that black lives and brown lives were such a threat that they'd become prey in the name of law and order set out by the king who was afraid he didn't look good enough wasn't smart enough so he [~~white out don't work here~~], not only on the street but every continent, flaming in the fear he'd never be mourned enough, not by his sister or his own sons—the story says the king set out to

all the born boys, the born baby boys, two and younger standing or face down arms up gunless and toothless in the wrong place at the wrong corner and for it came to pass, it came to pass that your amá hid you because the king was shaky at the knees afraid of a turn, una vuelta, revolución and you traveled across the border in the cover of night, your amá bent over hungry and scared and never sola, never la única amá who hid her child in her wrappings under the skin of the black and shimmering sky, and your apá on foot on guard both of them traveling on the word of an angel and a dream, dreamers all of 'em. This sorrow number two, flight to Egypt, flight from guns, slits, and clips and praying isn't enough for these sons and daughters but if I am praying this right, it should spill through the criss-cross fencing between the ages crush the criss-cross hell that is the cages, free the future kings and the future sages

Six Gawd

Black Girl Dies and is Resurrected

Black Girl dies and is resurrected
AKA: "we don't die; we multiply."
AKA
Every time I am pushed down watch me push through–
Concrete, gravel, rock, everything hard
See how I rise to the occasion
Exceeding everything you expected me to be
I am bigger than your imagination
The parts of me you've tried to kill
Tried to sacrifice for your gain
I am hard
Like the choices I've made to survive
Like trying over and over again
Despite hearing "no," "you can't," "stop".
Because no, I can't stop
Luxury
Life comes at such a high price
You don't want me to live
But you can't stop me
This is my body, my life
It's my choice
I will not allow you to kill my desire
This skin holds in a riot
A rage, an uprising, a passion for life
This world is not ready for my wrath
Luckily, I don't have the same taste for vengeance as you
The opposite of destruction is love
See how hard I love the broken pieces
See how strong they come together and build
You cannot shake me
I am already the ground you walk on
If you are not careful, I will be the black hole you fall in

Win

Ode to the Black Boy playing in the sprinkler in his front yard
.....I love you
Grow into a man
THRIVE
Change the world
Be the difference we so desperately need
Slam your fist into the walls and make them crumble
Break down the barriers designed to keep us out
And then Build from the broken
.....Again
Use the same foundation of this country
Broken spirits, broken families, broken hearts
Let it be *their* turn

Limit their opportunities, close doors in their faces
Let them know what it means to be naked
Show them what it means to fight but not conquer
What it feels like to speak but never be heard
Make them prove themselves..... constantly
Strip them of their privilege
Break them
Then celebrate
Celebrate the rebirth of a nation
Celebrate the rebirth of YOU

Find the balance
Be more saint than sinner
More justice and peace
Be more LOVE, more ONE
... Win

BUDDY WAKEFIELD

The Gift of My Hate

appears in *A Choir of Honest Killers*, Write Bloody Publishing, 2019

At the Concert for New York City in Madison Square Garden, five weeks after 9/11, Richard Gere stood in front of millions of viewers and said:

We have the possibility to turn this *horrendous energy*
we are all feeling from violence and revenge,
into compassion into love into understanding. *

The crowd
    booed him
                                     loudly
as if to say,
   Hey!
     Buddha Boy,

We will not be caught dead acting like Jesus Christ.

As if Christ only published concepts he wanted us to thump instead of experience.

Granted, *compassion* is a wounded word. It gets banged around in the junk drawer. It is not an entitled driver. Would not survive in California. Compassion is often the last player picked. So maybe Richard Gere should have used the word *rest* to suggest that we curb the poison of reacting so fast.

But journalists insisted Richard Gere's proposal for love and understanding was the *wrong time, wrong crowd, wrong message.* I remember being 27, watching this, feeling like some fathers do not tell their sons *I am proud of you*, like an entire city had learned the language of a well-disguised suicide smothered in clever headlines and a swarm of stagy news reporters who, years later, failed to mention that a French man named Antoine Leiris lost his wife, the mother of his child, with whom he was madly in love, to the terrorist attacks in Paris week before.
It was no more excruciating than what happened in
Baghdad, Beirut, or in the West Bank

during the same 24 hours. The difference
is that 5 days later
Antoine Leiris was the only man
to post a love letter for his son on the BBC,
an open message to those responsible for killing his wife.
He looked directly into their hungry little pain-bodies
and told them

I won't give you the gift of hating you.

         Pussy.
Pathetic propagandist.
  Candy-ass liberal. The insults
that followed Antoine's moment of peace made me
realize *Love* – wounded a word as it may be – *Love*
can see *all of it*, but *Anger* – is only concerned with what it
thinks is fair, narrow like the barrel of the NRA,
like the blueprints to Russia's femininity,
to China's childhood, to North Korea's private parts,
to the bruised music of the Confederate Flag states
still singing like a drunk Englishman
in a Tibetan monastery, loudly, louder, *Hey!*
I'm the Over-Compensator!
    The Great Annihilator!
Cross me, and you will know my pain!

In each of us
  lives a
small man
 with a
good heart
 and an
ego the size of
  Hitler.

Y'all, why are we not fighting fire with water?
Compassion will not make us lazy. It is okay to cross
these borders. It is okay to stay awake
to love our own ignorance enough to look at it square in
the wise guy, in the bright side, at the parts we are
terrified to acknowledge because of the work it will
probably cause us

because there is a chance we have been your own
terrorists. There's a chance we are a failed relationship.
There is a chance that every single day
we are the reason millions of animals actually
weep before slaughter and we do not get to
make up for it by watching adorable YouTube
videos while stuffing our face with their death.

It is more than some sellable cliché that – through these
bodies – we are rooted to the same source,that we have
arrived on this planet to experience form.
Now that we've had some time to do that, please,
let us reintroduce the idea of *questioning everything*.

Excessive packaging. Planned obsolescence. Breeding...Planned
obsolescence. Identity... Planned obsolescence. Your story...
Planned obsolescence. The narrative... Planned obsolescence.
Your story. Your narrative. Your identity. Fining people... Planned
Obsolescence. Question anything impractical... Finning people,
because they didn't have enough money in the first place. Question
everything impractical to the eradication of suffering.Like denying
refugees. Like putting a fence around freedom.Like the oceans of
care we keep for this world getting so landlocked in our chest that
when the answer tries moving over all the God dams built across our
flooded hearts to surprise us with consciousness, it might look like
we are spitting back entitlements at the Earth.

Stand down. Stay still. Gather your wits. Find their ends.
    Pull out the slack and say clearly,

Yes.

Compassion.

Love.

Understanding.

Go ahead.
Call me another cliché.
Stick your violence in my meditation.

The worst you can do to me for not joining
the gangland war on Christ's behavior
is shoot me in the look on my face, the one that says
I am not afraid to understand you. Or to stop you.

In *A New Earth*,
Eckhart Tolle describes us as the noisiest humans
in history. Some things do not need to be fact-checked.
Stop backing up so loudly. You screaming siren on a cell
phone. You heavy-footed upstairs neighbors.
Bloated bodies of anger belting out boos the size of
Madison Square Garden rejecting Richard Gere, who I
know very little about, but who I suspect, like most
humans, is part-saint, part-fraud, and who reporters had
to admit rebounded rather nicely when he acknowledged
what he had to offer was
apparently unpopular right now—

Like taking away your child's assault rifle.
Like the color white. Like the color brown.
Like supporting the man in Nigeria
who found the cure for HIV.
Unpopular is compassion.
Like a savings account in Greece.
Like the topic of trafficking Stockholm Syndrome
all the way back from New York City
to right here down the West of me
where I am determined to see all of it
because I don't get to go blind again,
not without carving the word *coward*
in holy brail
on every pen I will ever use
to point out how pain
cannot digest love.
It works the other way. My body
no longer loves writing poems for mass consumption.
It does not believe in blowing apart.

But I am still right here behind its habits,
stacks of ground down teeth and a
mashed-up forehead of rolling credits, working
to see all of it,

which I suspect is more productive
than giving you

the gift of my hate.

Zachary F. Caballero

On Showing Up in the Year 2020 in Not-So-Great America

In the United States of America,
the story goes
our country carved our rights
into a paper promise.
It was white men who told the world
we were created equal.
In this Not-So-Great-America,
words became law
by word of mouth
from the crooked teeth
of white men,
your and my
forefathers.
And like any bad father,
our country is bad at
keeping its promises.

If you have to say
Make America Great Again,
and
Keep America Great,
I want to ask—
whose greatness
do you wish to protect?

If going back in time
is your greatest wish,
what time is it?

Does your greatness
have a skin color?

What is
the color of a law?

What is a right
covered in blood?

What is a right
devoured by dark-money?
Institutional infiltration.
Corporate freedoms.
What is the right to speak
if the mouth is fictional,
and all it says are dollar signs?
Deep pockets and
false gods stack the odds,
rewriting laws into shadow talk
until it is impossible
to walk into a voting booth,
to immigrate into this county,
to walk the streets in protest
without the threat of police brutality
of murder, of innocent-before-guilty,
of state-sanctioned violence.
I could go on and on, but one month
for the presidential election
I choose hope. I choose the work
it takes to make tomorrow a better place.
Even if I do not always trust this place.
I choose hope.
Even if I do not know how I will
make it through the day.

Am I supposed to use my voice
to vote?
Or am I in a system
designed for me to lose?

Am I in a system
designed to choose for me?

In the fictional United States of America
set in the TV series *The West Wing*,
President Josiah "Jed" Bartlett tells an audience,
"Decisions are made by those who show up"

My friends, mi gente, mi familia—
apathy is the original sin
of every generation that
had a chance to choose
a better future.
In 2020, in Not-So-Great-America,
when the decisions are made,
who is going to decide for you?

RJ Wright

The Pledge

> *After Safia Elhillo*
> *Self-portrait with no flag*

I do not pledge allegiance to the flag of the United States of America
or any symbol that was not created with me in mind

Instead I pledge allegiance to the things that bring me joy and laughter
Like a toddler that wants me to watch them play

I pledge allegiance to things that make me who I am

I pledge allegiance to 90s cartoons

I pledge allegiance to corner boys and road mandem

I pledge allegiance to cross overs and jump shots

To free kicks and corner kicks to Manchester United and the Lakers

I pledge allegiance to kissing in school corridors
To kissing in empty classrooms
To kissing behind bike sheds

I pledge allegiance to my mouth/
Even when it resembles a haunted house/
Spilling over with the ghosts of former lovers
Who I have failed to pick from my gapped teeth/

I pledge allegiance to unrequited love

I pledged allegiance to a lot of things that are dead or dying

So, at one point all I pledged allegiance to was the United States of America,
I pledged allegiance to a lot of things that did not want me

Until I realized I'm worthy of loyalty of safety of love

I'm worthy of more than a noose
or a hashtag
or diversity hire
or a mass shooting,
or thoughts and prayers

So now pledge allegiance to my mother's hands

When she puts them together
She transforms into a mighty morphing pray warrior

I pledge allegiance to my bloodied and broken pride
That was shed so I might have life
And life more abundantly
Now don't that sound like communion

I pledge allegiance to ice cream in July and January because let's be honest
There is no bad time for ice cream

I pledge allegiance to 2am trips to Wal-Mart with friends
For no other reason than brown liquor
Because brown liquor makes everything seem like a good idea
At 2am

I pledge allegiance to the returning / to staying / to the never leaving
In the first place

I pledge allegiance to the people who prepare my food, to my Barber,
To my tattoo artist, to people who will fuck up my day
If I mistreat them

So that being said I pledge allegiance to my future wife, to our children,
To the staying, to the never leaving

I pledge allegiance to anything that will allow me to make a home of it

TOVA CHARLES

Reasons Why I Love Being Black

Dear God, Thank you for making me black.
Out of the rainbowed variation of people
I could be apart of ...
You still made me black
Mixed with black.

Damn **GOD...**
you a real one.

Even tho some
of your people try to make this black
sound like a bad dream or
Some kind of poison
Sitting at the bottom of an endless joke

But I just think they mad
Because you built them without rhythm
So they can't hear your heartbeat.

Thank you for giving me hair
That looks good
No matter what has been done to it.
And skin that won't burn

O **Alpha and Omega**
Why would you
let them burn like that?

That is a strange thing
to not protect your people from.

Thank you for making the universal call
Of black people
A trapped one.
One that if I hear it
I will know that my people are near.

Thank you for making yellow be the international color of black girls.

Thank you, Heavenly Father,
For Regina
And Beyonce
And Bun B
And 112
And Dru Hill
And Lauryn Hill
And the soul food soundtrack
And the waiting to exhale soundtrack
And for my black momma

Thank you **Waymaker** for making my momma both black and from the south.
Thank you for reminding me that the south ain't for everybody.
That I ain't for everybody
But we both fly anyhow

Thank you
for not just making me black
But a black girl from the south.
Thank you for making me all this fine and know how to cook gumbo.
And baked macaroni
Thank you for letting my flick of the wrist guide my food to seasoned perfection.

Thank you, King, of Kings and Lord of Lords,
for Chicken and watermelon
That we do not eat it in front of white people
Because they don't deserve to see how we break bread with our holiest of food.
Thank you for always making me proud
And black
And black
And black

Thank you
For making me funny
Thank you for helping me keep all the rage inside of a laugh
Thank you that laughter was the cure
Thank you for making my tongue as sharp as my nails
Thank you for making sure my words keep me alive ... for now
Amen

EMMY PÉREZ

Pandemic Solstice

first published in *The Langdon Review of the Arts in Texas, Tejascovido Edition*, Fall 2020

And so we will call this home
our heaven, our heaving,
our harm, and our justicia.

And yet we live, knowing
over 200,000+ in this country
dead and the George Floyd

mural in Brownsville
vandalized again,
knowing somewhere

someone is slurring
the n word and saying go back
to where you came from

as they believe their families
sprouted here like corn
ever since the very seeds

first grew on these plots of earth
they claim money and banks own.
I could write a polite sonnet,

sound my words, count syllables,
or I could choose to sing someone else's
love song instead. I could

paint my paint over the murals
of my papers like a palimpsest,
I could paint my pant, coat my tongue

with berries and fermented varieties
and see what messes I can create.
Poems can't change systems

and yet here I am refusing
to believe they can't charge
the synapses in my brain

with even some kind of minimal
protest to falling asleep
because dreams cannot

be recorded and sometimes the sun
shines longer than the moon.
This is a prelude to a protest,

a prelude to mourning
the voices, the appetites,
the people surviving COVID-19

but killed by others' hands
with guns and knees with kneelings-on
and chokeholds with their laws

and procedures that sanction.
We'll never cease our protests
because we were born

too soon in history's timeline
which means I have hope
for the future, if we can

also nurture the earth
while we are at it,
and I truly ask if that time

will ever come,
will that time ever come,
when will that time arrive

for everyone?

Sherrie "Candy" Zantea

Faith in You

I put so much faith in you that I had none left for myself.
What is a woman's tears worth? How the droplets are often confused with expensive perfume.
I've turned my body into a sanctuary for you. Yet you place other women idols at my altar,
poisoned my communion. And I am the one being passed over.
Me, being all woman. Fulfilled. A Donny Hathaway hymn lodged in my throat,
I tried to put Nina's spell on this relationship and just like sorcery you cursed me.
Constantly made me disappear,
Made the little girl in me stay hidden under covers
cause magical creatures and monsters are too much like chameleons.
The heart of a woman only knows care. Can only be distributor.
Only knows how to take fruit, woods and flowers and anoint your feet despite your fist.
Only knows worship on her knees despite your tongue.
I put so much faith in you, I forgot the teachings of my father. Both of them.
I put so much faith in you, I am a Samaritan woman drinking from an empty well, still trying to quench a man's thirst.
I put so much faith in you....I have none left for myself.
Treated you like Jesus, in return you made me your cross.
We both died on Calvary.
But I found the strength to resurrect
And Replenish all the faith I gave you with forgiveness.

AYOKUNLE FALOMO

Alternative

appears in *African, American*, winner of the New Delta Review Chapbook Contest, 2019

      SISTER, 18: *Do you know where they got the idea for zombies from?*
      BROTHER, 12: ▮▮▮▮▮?

I

Fact: Truth was. Truth is and will be
when all that ever was, is, and will be

ceases to be. Alternative Fact: Truth was.
Truth…will…cease to be. Alternative Fact be

an erasure of Truth. Fact, sturdy and upright as it be,
be a tree planted by the waters. It takes more than a wave

of its alternative for it to fall and find itself slanted
on the riverbank of that which we know for certain.

And it is certain that a fruit does not fall too far
from the tree that it belongs to. What I mean is

I've heard it said that Satan be the father of lies,
and Truth never birthed no alternative to claim as a son, so…

What is Truth if not that which refuses to leave its root
to be carried away with the wind! And we all have seen

it – what the wind can do! It, beast of burden that it is,
carries on its back everything; knows how to transport

to our ears a lie
from where it's made a home in the mouths
of those whose tongues find truth an unwelcome guest.

What a journey!!

II

November 8, 2016 ---

America woke up dressed in its true colors. I look at the map, adorned by 58% white, and all I saw was red. I slept with the blue that overwhelmed me upon realizing that 58% of America couldn't wait for the White House to throw up, I mean throw out all the melanin it's been stained with and instead, have the orange puppet run his tiny hands across its walls;

I woke up to a new dawn, except there was nothing new about the dawn. I mean that it dawned on me upon waking up that there is nothing new about any of this. I mean that I woke up with leaking faucets for eyes. I mean I woke up, and America hates this. I woke up, even though in a puddle…and America loves this, asks if it can join and take a swim.

III

Alternative be a magician,

looks history in its face and turns it into something that isn't,
or rather makes of what isn't a thing for us all to mourn;

reminds us all to mourn in remembrance of those
whose breath the morning couldn't account for

but refuses to name their bodies;

is silent in the face of actual tragedy and when
questioned, asks: what stench? What bodies?

Instead, gives a tragedy that isn't
a name, calls it the Bowling Green Massacre
except there are no bodies in the coffin to mourn

Truth dies at the hands of an imposter and
no one shows up to mourn its demise.

Its alternative shows up to the funeral
and turns it into a celebration,

brings along thousands of people,
like those who apparently showed up to

██████'s inauguration even though
their bodies did not come with them.

IV

I've heard

my people say: *bi iro ba lo fun ogun odun, otito yio ba lojo kan*
Translation: a lie can travel for 20 years but one day, the truth will
find it! Translation: we need not ask or be on the long search for

where Truth is
as long as
we still have

our voices.

Glori B

Solidarity

Today, I want to tell you the story
of the first time I realized voting was important.

                       (No, it isn't in 2008, or in 2012, or even 2016-
                  This isn't a presidential election, or even a midterm-)

The year is 1999. I am in sixth grade,
and I am obsessed
with MTV's *TRL*.

Now I know many of you may not have been born in 1999,
so I'll try to help you out with some modern day comparisons.

TRL was a countdown show- viewers voted by phone-
           (no, not with a text message, or an app- we didn't have those.)
A phone call, like when you talk to your grandmother,
but the phone plugged into the wall-
Or you could even vote online-
           (like a facebook poll, but that was the whole website, just that poll?)

And the show, *Total Request Live*, or *TRL*
was hosted by Carson Daly –
                  (who you know from *The Voice* or *The Today Show*,
                         but at the time he was kind of hot?)

Anyway, so people would vote for the best music video
so they could watch it on the show, live that afternoon
               (and like, we didn't have YouTube so we couldn't just…
               watch whatever video we wanted, so if you liked a video
                  you had to get it on the show so you could watch it,)
and sometimes if it was #7 or #3 they would only play a clip
but the #1 song, they always played the whole video.

TRL started in September of 1998—
and I watched it every single day that year—
and every single damn day
the number one song was either
by the Backstreet Boys or N*Sync.

(And if you don't know what that is,
they aren't even different bands really,
imagine two bands made of 5 Justin Biebers,)

((and sure, one of them is Justin Timberlake,
but we didn't know that yet so it doesn't count.))

Every day.
For Months.

The top song every day
went to these whiny white boys
in loose fitting, light-washed denim

and if you liked anything resembling Rock music
it was very hard to see your band's music videos
(because again, no cell phone, no YouTube, no TiVo.)

And in sixth grade, my favorite band was Orgy.
(No, I didn't know what that word meant at the time.)
And that's not what's important,
what's important is that my favorite band was weird
and they didn't have a shot at the top 10.
I knew that as much as I wanted "Blue Monday"
to be the number one song on *TRL*
that it was never going to happen-
that no matter how many times I voted,
there weren't enough other people who felt the way I did—
and this is not the last time in my life
that I have voted for something
knowing it has no shot at winning.

So, I knew my number one would never be number one,
But it seemed equally impossible that number one
would even ever be something I could stomach.

But then, Korn's "Freak on a Leash" made the top 10.
(If you don't know what Korn is,
imagine 5 guys who would look like mumble rappers now,
but playing heavy guitar and screaming upsetting lyrics.)
And we were shocked that this video made the top 10.

But it rose.
And it rose.
Every day.
because all the weirdos
were banding together
to surge the voting every day.

Voting for Korn wouldn't get Orgy on the top 10,
but it would displace the dueling denim dudes.

And literally- on my twelfth birthday- we did it.

Korn's "Freak on a Leash"
was the number one music video in the country
on my twelfth birthday,
and it made the top spot seven more times
from February to April
beating N*Sync
and Brittney Spears
and The Backstreet Boys
again and again

and it is then that I learned what solidarity can do.

I have one vote. And it is not much.
I have one voice. And it is not much.
But there are a lot of weirdos in this world.
And together, we are a megaphone.

> ((Imagine
> what we could change
> if we all screamed

at the same time.))

Haikus

Just like handwashing
voting's most effective if
everyone does it

Yeah, I'm voting for
the lesser of two evils.
'cause it's LESS evil

A journey of a
thousand victories begins
with a single vote

Voting won't fix it,
but it will give us the tools
to start the repairs

We all need to vote
like our lives depend on it:
cause this time…they do

Voter suppression
efforts are rampant this year:
vote for those who can't.

Don't think your vote counts?
Well, it certainly doesn't
if you don't cast it.

Armando "AXL" Lopez

Su Voto Es Su Voz

It is a simple motto.
Your vote is your voice!
The polling place is a sanctuary.
Enter the sacred place.

Once you have the ballot in front of you.
Nothing can stop your freedom roar.
With push of a button or the mark of a pencil,
Your inner voice echoes forever.

This is the lasting mark of democracy.
It is the sword that slays despots.
It is the weapon of the humble.
It is the shield to carry out the oppressor.

The path to the vote is our history.
Spilled blood paints the way
Of a declaration of independence unfulfilled,
Seeking the inclusion of the metaphorical "all men."

The heroes of this democratic promise beckon you.
The heroines of the growth of our union invite you.
Listen to their voices in the air.
"This is the voice that would be denied to you."

Enter this vociferous movement with us.
Register so that you are not excluded.
Be vigilant of the date and time and place.
Let your voice and their voices be heard.

Su voto es su voz!

Eternalmente!

What Are They Afraid Of?

Let us gather in a patriotic session.
To march in this glorious procession
To those whose goal is voter suppression.
We are aware of your systemic oppression.
Each decade continues dangerous aggression.
Limit the vote to white men with landed possession.
When slavery is abolished begin the laws of discretion.
Literacy tests, poll taxes and laws to prevent accession.
Gender restrictions intent on stunting political egression.
Conspiracies to limit worker access by voting day compression.
When all these steps would fail, there was simple violent repression.
So much fear of full voter participation allowing a true citizen expression.
Such are the machinations of those intent on controlling our nation's succession.

Paul Wilkinson Jr.

One Eat A

they never told us that we couldn't vote
that our rights
had been mislabeled and mislocated
because then
they would have to admit that they were wrong

no

they told us we could vote
but then tried to convince us that our vote didn't matter

somehow
our amplified voices were only heard in an echo chamber

i
remember
talking to my grandmother and saying that voting
was passive in the face of aggression

it was like spitting on a forest fire
or yelling at god to turn down the august sun

i told her that i don't vote because voting doesn't change things
i felt the winner
was always predetermined in a room full of men that would never value my ideas
and the loser
was always me

i told her that voting
only pacified the people
left us holding a bag of half filled promises

i remember
talking to my grandmother while anger
was climbing up my soul and running off my tongue

i told her that i don't vote because our vote didn't matter

but my grandmother
never argued with me
never tried to make me feel unvalidated
never left my feelings unheard

she just asked if i was hungry
then told me that she votes
but not for the count

she votes because her mother couldn't

no one wanted to know what her mother thought

she told me that she votes
because someone wants her not to

someone thinks she isn't smart enough to direct her own path

she told me that she votes because when my grandfather died
the city council had an ordinance that he had to be buried in the back of
the cemetery
because even in death he was disrespected

she told me that she votes
because if her vote didn't matter
there wouldn't be people trying to stop it today

today
i vote
because my grandmother made me feel validated
and reminded me that i don't just vote for me

but i vote
because my grandparents
are no longer able to

i vote for them
and for my sons and daughters

i vote for us

Natasha Carrizosa

today, i will begin again

as the seed
shadow sewn
enveloped in uncertainty
submerged in dreams
deferred
whispering/wandering
am i?

i am

my mother
is
lion
earth
my father
be
feather
on the lamb
unheard
either way
i turn
or run
i am
plume
of my makers

it is written
i will begin again
i must have faith
i am destined for greatness

today, i will begin again
to remember myself
to grow beyond
the glass ceiling
of disbelief
of trauma
of self-doubt

of negative thoughts
of the cannot
of the impossibilities
of the atrocious
of the atrophy

it is written
i will begin again
i must prune my own weeds
i am destined for greatness

today, i will begin again
growing (slowly)
knowing (seeking)
moving (mountains)
unfolding (truth)
unfinished (creation)
pressing forward (first. kings. something.)
crowning (is. everything.)
i am destined for greatness

today, i will begin again
be coming
be patient
be loving
be sun
bathing
be music
listening
be bird
watching
be smoke
praying
be humble
eight-seventeen
bumblebee sting
remembering
be still
my beating heart
be no longer
suffering
sacrificing

sanctimonious

today, i will begin again

i am just
a seed
kin to cloud
kneeling
begging sun
for a way out

i must hold on
i must be (mustard seed)
i am small (thought)
i am better (now)
i am reaching (out)
i might be
poet
tree

i am grounded
i am destined for greatness

today, i will begin again
breathing
speaking
remembering
the language of my heart

today, i will begin again
i am
destined for greatness

it is written

pepper belly

(or, spittin' chile)

i will never forget
first time i was called
pepper belly
black girl
(R L Paschal High School)
i thought was my sister
(chile. pronounced: ch isle)

(tasha. be cool.)

i will never forget
first time i was called
nigger
brown boy
(De Zavala Elementary School)
i thought was my brother
(chile. pronounced chee leh)

(natasha. be cool.)

what should i do?
be?
say?

as a)
black girl
brown woman
poet
might be
always in

b) between

black
brown
blood

c) divine

baptism
chest
(chile) (long i)
flood (eyes)

i am equal parts
pac angelou
i rose bloom
concrete
when i cry
still i rise

i am equal parts
lotería cards
el negrito
la sirena
hecho a mano
(grito. griot.)

they called me:

mutt
heinz 57
nigger
flagpole
llanta
¿como se dice
aguanta en inglés?
wetback
mono

monkey

white boy one time
chemistry class
saw some 7-11 coffee
spilled
on my white t- shirt
in front of class
he asked:
i always wondered if black girls
gave chocolate milk

he and the white man
teacher
laughed

yes i am
spittin' chile
sí soy chile

peppers
in my belly

SHEILA BLACK

November

You won't come soon enough for Marie to keep
her car or Jed not to lose his health insurance.

You won't come soon enough for us to forget
the man with a mouth like a door with a nail in it

or the children he took from their mothers
to lock in cages in the bone-dry of desert where

the nights freeze the water in the metal taps
and no charity blanket printed with spacemen or

rabbits is enough to hold back the bad dreams.
You won't come soon enough to clear the air

of the fires burning or to stop the virus from shattering
another unwitting family. You won't come soon

enough for the damage to be undone, but this is a road
we know we must make with our feet—one in

front of the other—and we are ready for marching.
You won't come soon enough to break down the wall

before it stops another person cold, at a river they never
wanted to cross. But we can dig this river with our hands

so the water flows again freely between us, slightly warm
to the touch, like our skin, like our skins,

like our breath, which, even here, we learn links us in an
unbreakable chain, and when you come, we will be ready.

"When 4 am Dark is Narrow I Feel It"

Lately, the longing for sleep as if
it would return me to the real before
our lungs became a fraught network.
Maybe we will have learned to breathe
together or that we do. Instead on
the computer I warm up with a whir,
unlike the bang of the boiler I remember
from the other years, pictures of a city
burning for 100 days. When I talk to
Dwayne over Zoom and I try to say this
is different, he gives me a look that is
weariness mostly. He says, "Think," and he
sketches with his hands a wheel; it
has been this way and again, and the
bridge with the dogs he names and
Abner Louima held in the bowels
of the New York Subway, brutalized
beyond any reasonable imagining.
What do we do it for? I am thinking a lie
I told myself a long time ago, which
was that no one meant me harm. An
obvious lie since I told it to my mother
at the edge of a playground where for
months a few boys had circled each
morning, sometimes with stones. They
used the words people have used for eons
to describe a body like mine – crippled,
but also witch, also cursed, also "God
must hate you, because God hates what
is ugly." One of these boys. after my surgery
when they broke each leg seven times
and refitted them into straighter lines
said, "They may have tried to change you
but you are still ugly." Now in the charcoal
light of fires doused and reset, stamped down,
like mine to go underground and flare again
in a wheel that burns off only pain, only
grief, I try to peer into that lie. Was it fear
that lived in those faces or the older animal

impulse of running in a pack so fast a
world blurred as you took down, took in
another life —as if in recompense
for having been so ever-hungry—but for
what? The machine whirs hot with pictures
of a burning Target and people around taking
what they can as if in recompense for wilder
hungers. What did I want but to break like sun,
to have a person smile at me as if I were all
joy. What could I do with difference but
hold it up like a crystal that could shape a
light until it bent in my direction. I want
to believe it is possible to change. I want
to think about the lungs we share and that breath
which passes from one to the next, that
breathe we take and we give.

Vocab "Andrea" Sanderson

Hard Won

A lyric poem for the centennial celebration of the 19th Amendment and Women's Suffrage

>This is a hard won and we're not done.
>Let's roll up our sleeves, and climb this mountain.
>This is a hard won and we're not done.
>Let's roll up our sleeves, and get this job done.

I found my growl. I found my grit. Time to take a stand.
I cannot sit or crouch timidly in the shadows,
my heart wanting and void of sound.
Can't keep looking for promise in darkness,
hoping my light would be found.
So I am sending out a beacon to illuminate the barren ground.
I'm seeking sisterhood from the furthest corners.
May justice tear all the borders down.
Silent Sentinels protest with nature's force
if we join together, we can change the course of history.
Rallies and protests create a collage of resistance.
No matter the challenges faced we will persist. This is-
the tip of the iceberg melting away.
My power is crawling to the surface.
I have so much to say. My voice is no longer worthless.

>This is a hard won and we're not done.
>Let's roll up our sleeves, and climb this mountain.
>This is a hard won and we're not done.
>Let's roll up our sleeves, and get this job done.

The Suffrage movement trickled to women of color, but it shouldn't silence any daughters or mothers. Women of every nationality and creed should be respected equally.
Hard Won.

SARAH MADDUX

Y'all

The girl on the Boston T
with the nose piercing and pink pussy hat says
"Yeah, if the Northern states could just succeed from the Southern states,
That would be great."

And so I did what Southerners do.
I spoke up,
Ever so politely to tell her,
  "We're not all the same."

There was so much else I wanted to say,
Like
"Are you willing to abandon the majority of the people of color in this country as long as your fate isn't tied to theirs?"
Like
"While slaves picked cotton in Georgia and Mississippi, the blood money siphoned from their backs flowed into banks in New York City."
Like
"Do you think living in this lily white New England bubble means that you're not complicit in the atrocities that our ancestors committed?
Like
Do you know how hard we fight in the South?
Across picket lines?
Across family dinner tables?
The South has always been the battleground for this country's soul
While the North pretended not to see that there was blood on their hands too.

When Northerners use exaggerated Southern accents as a proxy for stupidity or ignorance
I feel my own fragile accent curl inside me like a dying flower
Mine only ever blooms inside my Grandmama's kitchen
Her accent is a yellow rose, all curving notes and curling edges
Mine is a dandelion,
Brittle,
Blown away at the slightest pressure
Southern kids know we have to carve the hayseed out of our tongues
If we ever want to be taken seriously

I am a dilution of my own culture
Stripped of all my rough edges
And scrubbed of Southern soil
To gain entrance to this ivory tower

It a complicated thing to be a Southerner
To hold so much pride and shame and anger in the same heart
It all becoming intertwined so that we can't tell them apart anymore
Raising monuments to long dead confederate heroes
Clinging blindly to a false version of our past we do not have to wince at.

But if we could just get through that pain
Face ourselves as we are now
We'd find we have so much else to be proud of.

Did you know that the term 'redneck'
Referred to the red bandanas Appalachian miners wore over their faces
When they rose up in defiance of exploitative mining companies?

Have you heard of the cajun navy
Who tote their fishing boats from state to state
To rescue people from hurricane choked cities
When FEMA can't be bothered to show up?

Did you know that Houston, Texas is the most diverse city in the country?
With more than 140 languages spoken daily in its humid streets

And what would you do without the music and art that grew out of our blood-stained soil?
Willie Nelson and Otis Redding
Outkast and The Chicks
Johnny Cash and Selena
Dolly Parton and Missy Elliot

And then there's the food
We've got fried chicken and enchiladas and gumbo
And cornbread and and barbecue and sweet potato pie
What's Boston got...clam chowder?

We're proud of the word "y'all"
Because it's efficient, inclusive, and gender neutral,
Y'all!

The South has never been just one thing.
We are not a melting pot;
We're chili
And jambalaya
And menudo
All at once

So to the girl on the train in Boston,
Take it from a Southerner
Succession doesn't end well
We're all on this wild ride together
And if that ever changes,
We're keeping Beyonce.

Shaggy

Puff, Puff, Vote!

If you want one more way to fight racism, get high!
And I don't mean that as blunt stunting, riff spliffing, doobie Scoobing
Hot boxing stoner
But as a blunt stunting, riff spliffing, doobie Scoobing
Hot boxing stoner who knows his history!
You see, less than a hundred years ago, marijuana
Was legal in the United States
And while you couldn't buy it at the corner store or from the ice cream man
Like you can today in my neighborhood
You could- in the right city from the right person-
Legally purchase the dankest glow in the darkest
Stickiest ickiest wickiest thickiest Kind imaginable
Capitalism at its finest as people were making money with the weed
And with that money gaining power
And with that power gaining the ability to better their lives and fight those who abused their own power
The system was about to be rocked until America- in the 1930s- woke up and remembered…hey, we're fucking racist
Capitalism is not for those kind of people
And this gateway merchandise
A legal gateway to money
jobs
success
middle class
upper class
power
acceptance
and more
Has to be stopped
So a government official, the man ultimately in charge of who says
Alcohol: Good. Marijuana: Evil, said this:
"Reefer makes $#%*&%@^ think they're as good as white men.
Their Satanic music, jazz and swing, result from marijuana use."
And then to further tap into America's genetic racism
He terrified the white people with horror stories of murder and rape
Marijuana was so insidious that, quote: "If the hideous monster Frankenstein came face to face with marijuana, he would drop dead of fright!"

Weed is obviously not illegal for health reasons
I can drive five miles and buy a fried chicken sandwich with bacon
add extra bacon
cheese
add extra cheese
mayonnaise
add extra mayonnaise
include a side of Ranch to dip the sandwich in
and instead of bread
the only slightly healthy thing in the whole sandwich
I can get two more pieces of fried chicken instead

It ain't about the health
And it ain't about the crime because that was non-existent before possession itself became the crime

No, the worst thing that happens when you get infected with the Reefer Madness is, even if its two in the morning and you are in your pajamas, you will drive five miles, slowly
in order to buy a fried chicken sandwich with bacon
add extra bacon
cheese
add extra cheese
mayonnaise
add extra mayonnaise
fuck the lettuce and tomato
include a side of Ranch to dip the sandwich in
and instead of bread
the only slightly healthy thing in the whole sandwich,
I can get two more pieces of fried chicken- or two donuts!- instead

And this is another reason why Colin Kaepernick does not need to stand for the national anthem

146 .... Contra

Contributing Authors' Bios

Omer Ahmed

Omer Ahmed (Pronouns: He/Him) is a Black and Muslim educator, writer, and performer. He has works published in issues or forthcoming issues of *The Sonora Review*, *The Penn Review* and internationally in *Bareknuckle Poet* amongst other places. Omer currently works for Writers in the Schools and hopes to expand his love of writing to further audiences, with a high focus on the youth.

Glori B

Glori B. is the stage name of Gloria C. Adams, a poet, teacher, mother, and leader in the Austin slam scene. She has competed on Final Stage at the National Poetry Slam, the Women of the World Poetry Slam, and Texas Grand Slam and is a three-time National Haiku Head-to-Head Champion. She is the author of seven chapbooks, and her work can be found on YouTube and Facebook video via Write About Now.

Wendy Barker

Wendy Barker's seventh collection of poetry is *Gloss* (Saint Julian Press, 2020). Her sixth collection, *One Blackbird at a Time*, received the John Ciardi Prize for Poetry (BkMk Press, 2015). Her fifth chapbook is *Shimmer* (Glass Lyre Press, 2019). An anthology of poems about the 1960s, *Far Out: Poems of the '60s*, co-edited with Dave Parsons, was released by Wings Press in 2016. Other books include a selection of poems with accompanying essays, *Poems' Progress* (Absey & Co., 2002), and a selection of translations, *Rabindranath Tagore: Final Poems* (co-translated with Saranindranath Tagore, Braziller, 2001). Her poems have appeared in numerous journals and anthologies including *The Southern Review*, *Nimrod*, *New Letters*, *Poetry*, *Prairie Schooner*, and *Plume*, as well as The Best American Poetry 2013. She is the author of *Lunacy of Light: Emily Dickinson and the Experience of Metaphor* (Southern Illinois University Press, 1987), as well as co-editor (with Sandra M. Gilbert) of *The House is Made of Poetry: The Art of Ruth Stone* (Southern Illinois University Press, 1996). Recipient of NEA and Rockefeller fellowships among other awards, she is the Pearl LeWinn Endowed Chair and Poet-in-Residence at the University of Texas at San Antonio, where she has taught since 1982.

Gregg Barrios

Gregg Barrios is a San Antonio playwright, poet, and journalist. He is a 2018 Yale Fellow and a 2019 National Endowment of the Humanities Fellow.

Sheila Black

Sheila Black is the author of four poetry collections, most recently *Iron, Ardent* (Educe Press, 2017). A fifth collection *Vivisection* is forthcoming from Salmon Poetry. She is a co-editor of *Beauty is a Verb: The New Poetry of Disability* (Cinco Puntos Press, 2011). Her poems have appeared in *Poetry*, *The Birmingham Review*, *The New York Times* and other places. She lives in San Antonio, Texas, and works for AWP.

Kevin Burke

Since moving to Austin from the southland of Chicago over ten years ago, Kevin W. Burke has become a staple in the Texas poetry community. In the arena of competitive poetry, Kevin is the 2011 Austin Poetry Slam Champ, 2011 Southwest Shootout Slam Champ, and a two-time Texas GrandSlam Poetry Festival Champion (2011 & 2013). He is the founder and president of Timber Mouse Publishing and aside from three DIY chapbooks, his own work has been previously published by *Freeze Ray Press*, *Into Quarterly*, Timber Mouse Publishing (album), and Button Poetry (video). Most recently, his first full length collection entitled *Going Down Singing* was published by Write About Now Publishing and Timber Mouse Publishing (2019).

Outside of the world of poetry, Kevin is the lead vocalist of County Hell, works as a firefighter, and lives just south of Austin where he and his spouse host events that provide performance space for poets and musicians out of their home, The Fresh Mint House.

Zachary Caballero

Zachary Caballero is a first-generation Texas Trial Lawyer, public speaker, and nationally recognized Mexican-American poet whose poems and performances have been featured on Huff Post Latino Voices as one of the Top 10 Spoken Word Poets who Speak to Diverse Latino Issues, We are Mitú', Button Poetry, Write About Now, Freeze Ray Press, and at the 2016 Austin International Poetry Festival. Zachary has been part of the Texas spoken word community for over a decade, and in that time has competed at the National Poetry Slam 4 times, taught writing and performing workshops across Texas, co-founded Spitshine Poetry at the University of Texas-Austin in 2011, and was crowned Write About Now's 2016 Grand Slam Poetry Champion.

Natasha Carrizosa

Natasha Carrizosa (Natty) is black and brown. Permanent marker. Poet/Writer/Seeker of truth always. She loves reggae music, sitting amongst the trees, Presidente brandy, and clove clouds. She might be a vibe. She cannot stand 45.

Tova Charles

Tova Charles, a powerhouse performing spoken word artist that has been taking the Slam community by storm since 2008. Born in Lafayette, LA but raised in Austin, TX. The daughter of a Librarian and Zydeco Percussionist, life was never boring. She gained her passion for writing from her mother and her passion for performing from her father. In spring 2003 she had the pleasure of being inducted in Sigma Gamma Rho Sorority, Inc., one of the original Historically Black Sororities. She is not only a great writer, performer and human being. She has also work as the Creative director for They Speak, Austin's premier youth poetry slam with the late Dr. Sheila Siobhan. She plans on continuing her career as a Spoken word artist and as an activist in the youth poetry movement. She has performed all over the country and has participated in national Slams including: 2009 National Poetry Slam, Placing 5th overall, 2010 National Poetry Slam, Semi-Finalist • 2010 Southwest Shoot out • Finalist of 2010 Rock The Republic Festival, 2010 Slam Champ of the University of Houston Scarlet Poetry Slam Team, Finalist of 2011 Woman of the World Poetry Slam, Placing 10th overall. She has release two books: *Handled with Care* and *Quiet, the voices in my head have something to say* with a new book is coming soon. She is a Graduate of the University of Houston with a BA in English Lit and currently teaching 6th Grade Writing and the mother to the amazing Harper Charles.

Vincent Cooper

Vincent Cooper is the author of *Zarzamora – Poetry of Survival* and *Where the Reckless Ones Come to Die*. His poetry can be found in *Somos En Escrito, Boundless*, and *Whatever Keeps the Lights On*.

Tarfia Faizullah

Tarfia Faizullah was born in Brooklyn, New York, to Bangladeshi immigrants and raised in Texas. She is the author of two poetry collections, *Registers of Illuminated Villages* (Graywolf, 2018) and *Seam* (SIU, 2014). Her writing has appeared widely in the US and abroad in the *Daily Star, BuzzFeed, Hindu Business Line, Huffington Post, Ms. Magazine, The New Republic, The Nation, Oxford American, Poetry*, and the Academy of American Poets website, as well as in the anthology *Halal If You Hear Me* (Haymarket, 2019) and the television show *PBS News Hour*.

The recipient of a Fulbright fellowship, three Pushcart prizes, and other honors, Faizullah presents work at institutions and organizations worldwide, and has been featured at the Liberation War Museum of Bangladesh, the Library of Congress, the Smithsonian, the Rubin Museum of Art, the Fulbright Conference, the Lannan Center for Poetics and Social Practice, the Radcliffe Seminars, New York University, Barnard College, University of California Berkeley, the Poetry Foundation, the Clinton School of Public Service, Brac University, and elsewhere.

Faizullah's writing has been translated into Bengali, Persian, Chinese, and Tamil, and was included in the theater production *Birangona: Women of War*. Her collaborations include photographers, producers, composers, filmmakers, musicians, and visual artists, resulting in several interdisciplinary projects, including an EP, *Eat More Mango*. In 2016, Harvard Law School included Faizullah in their list of 50 Women Inspiring Change.

Ayokunle Falomo

Ayokunle Falomo is Nigerian, American, and the author of *African, American* (New Delta Review, 2019) and two self-published collections. A recipient of fellowships from Vermont Studio Center and MacDowell, his work has been featured in/on Write About Now, *The New York Times*, Houston Public Media, *Michigan Quarterly Review*, *The Texas Review* and elsewhere. He holds a Bachelor of Science degree in Psychology from University of Houston, a Specialist in School Psychology degree from Sam Houston State University and is currently a Master of Fine Arts (Poetry) student at the University of Michigan's Helen Zell Writers' Program.

Anel I. Flores

Anel I. Flores is a lesbian, queer, woman story maker. Her work manifests itself as drawings, chapters, and poems, as a continuation and evolution of the conversations started by the Xicana movement in art and literature, now infused by latinx, transfeminism, intersectionality, queer politics and resistance. As a cultural producer, Flores is driven by a sense of urgency to record and create queer visual and literary work as a continuous reflection and questioning of self-representation, aiming at discovering and recovering the history, dynamics, and complexities of relationships with others, self, memory, future the present. Flores' areas of study and production of literary fiction and visual art center around Chicana/Latina literature, lesbianidad, sexuality, gender, race/border/diaspora, spirituality, body, blood memory and their connection to identity. She is an MFA in Creative Writing. She is Co-Reviewer and Co-Committee Member of El Mundo Zurdo Conference organized by the Society for the Study of Gloria Anzaldúa, Board Member of Macondo Writer's Workshop, Founder of Queer Voices Speak Out, Co-Founder of LezRideSA, and a member of the San Antonio Mayor's LGBTQIA Task Force. Flores was awarded Best Local Poet, Women's Advocate of the Year 2018 from University of Texas San Antonio, the Nebrija Creadores Award from the Universidad de Alcalá de Henares in Madrid, Spain, was named Best Of San Antonio Local Author 2017 and Best of San Antonio Local Poet 2020, the Chingona in Literature Award 2016, the Ancinas Award at Squaw Valley, the NALAC Fund for the Arts Award, the Accion Women Inspiring Women Award, the Yellow Rose of Texas Educator Award, and the Mentorship

Leadership Award from the National Performance Network. Most recently her artwork was exhibited at the McNay Museum, The Tex Pop Museum and Centro de Artes. During her 25-year career as an artist, Flores' work has been showcased at galleries, universities, and in academic journals. She is co-editor of forthcoming *Jota Anthology* with Korima Press and author of Lambda literary award nominated book *Empanada: A Lesbiana Story en Probaditas*. Among various anthologies and magazines, Flores' work can be found in *Camino Real*, *The Fifth Wednesday Journal*, *RiverSedge Literary Journal*, *Entre Guadalupe y Malinche: Tejanas in Literature and Art* with UT Press, *The Jota Anthology*, *Queer Spiritualities*, *Rooted: A Queer Women of Color Anthology*, *El Mundo Zurdo Anthology*, *The Brillantina Project*, *Sinister Wisdom*, *This City Is A Poem*, *Raspa Magazine*, *OutInSA Magazine*, *Iungo Arts Magazine*, *The Lodestar Quarterly*, *The Pitkin Literary Review* and *La Voz de Esperanza*. Her play *Empanada* toured for 8+ years throughout the University and Theater circuit and continues to be produced today. In 2019, Flores was interviewed by the Jotxs y Recuerdos podcast, the MALCS Journal podcast among others. She is currently in the process of completing her forthcoming book, *Cortinas de Lluvia*, a series of Children's books and a graphic memoir titled, *Pintada de Rojo*. Her teaching career includes 11 years in public high school, college, and university along with 4 years in Arts Administration, and various community literary workshops.

Six Gawd

Six Gawd is a 31-year-old queer black poet, hailing from San Antonio, Texas. A lover of words, craft beer, and women, not necessarily in that order. She writes for the same reasons a caged bird sings. She hopes that you might just listen. As the founder and owner of The Spice Rack, her personal practice is in encouraging specifically women of color to "survive". Six Gawd introduces herself as a "survivor" and promotes "all women of color are survivors when we make it to the next day in a world that institutionally treats us an afterthought.

Rodney Gomez

Rodney Gomez was born and raised in Brownsville, Texas. He serves as the 2020-2021 McAllen, Texas Poet Laureate. His poetry collections include *Arsenal* with Praise Song (Orison Books, 2021), *Geographic*

Tongue (Pleiades Press, 2020), winner of the Pleiades Press Visual Poetry Series, *Ceremony of Sand* (YesYes Books, 2019), and *Citizens of the Mausoleum* (Sundress Publications, 2018). His work appears in *Poetry, New England Review, The Gettysburg Review, North American Review, Verse Daily*, and other journals. His chapbook *Mouth Filled Night* won the Drinking Gourd Prize from Northwestern University's Poetry and Poetics Colloquium.

In 2020 he was awarded an Academy of American Poets Poet Laureate Fellowship "given to honor poets of literary merit appointed to serve in civic positions and to enable them to undertake meaningful, impactful, and innovative projects that engage their fellow residents, including youth, with poetry, helping to address issues important to their communities". Gomez' time as poet laureate is centered on an anthology of RGV youth poetry, the establishment of a poetry workshop which will encourage and develop young poets, a poet laureate website, and an RGV poetry map. Rigoberto González has called Gomez a poet with a "remarkable vision" whose work "celebrates the borderlands, its strangeness and its stark beauty".

Aris Kian

Aris Kian is an aspiring student of community organizing and abolition. She is ranked #10 in the 2020 Women of the World Poetry Slam and #4 at CUPSI with CoogSlam in 2019. She is an Emerging Writers Fellow with Writers in the Schools and an Inprint C. Glenn Cambor Fellow at the University of Houston. Currently, she explores work surrounding her experience with academia, critical theory, and the Black imagination.

Armando "AXL" Lopez

Armando X. Lopez has been a practicing attorney in Laredo, Texas for 37 years. He is happily married to Mary Lou Mendiola Lopez, a curriculum coordinator for the United Independent School District. They have three adult children, Mara Lorena Lopez, Armando M. Lopez, and Alejandro X. Lopez and are the proud grandparents of Melina Lamar Maldonado and Romina Meabh Lopez.

In addition to owning and writing for *The Laredo Sports Journal* from 1997 to 2001, Armando has also written for *The Laredo News LareDos*,

The Laredo Morning Times, The San Antonio Express and other publications. He is a current member of the boards of the Laredo Center for The Arts, Laredo Border Slam, the Laredo Institute For Theatrical Education AKA L.I.T.E Productions and is a member of the City of Laredo Fine Arts Commission. He has previously served on the board of the Laredo Bar Association and was past president of Leadership Laredo.

Armando is a writer who has had two of his plays performed at the Laredo Little Theater. His poetry has been published by the Guadalupe Cultural Arts Center in San Antonio as part of its Conjunto Festival. He has been a poet with Laredo Border Slam since 2012 and performed with Laredo Border Slam in Laredo, San Antonio, Houston, Tulsa, and Baton Rouge.

Sarah Maddux

Maddux is currently pursuing her PhD in immunology at the University of Pennsylvania and spends her time pining for a good taco. She writes about science, her family, and the experience of womanhood. She's been on several slam poetry teams and published in various anthologies, but her real passion is for the community that poetry creates. She also enjoys board games, horror movies, and baking.

Ryan McMasters

Ryan McMasters is an internationally published poet out of Pasadena, Texas. He has work published in The City of Houston's website, Ireland's *HCE Review, Peculiar Journal, Shiela-Na-Gig Journal, Moon Tide Press, Allegory Ridge,* the *San Antonio Review,* and *Show Bear Family Circus.*

Bill Moran

Bill Moran is a performance poet and former medic from Houston, TX. He is a two-time Austin Poetry Slam Champion and has an MFA Poetry degree from Louisiana State University. He has toured regularly since 2011, performing and teaching throughout the UK, Europe, Australia, Southeast Asia, and the US. He currently teaches creative writing in Houston for Writers in the Schools, and his solo debut book *Oh God Get Out Get Out* is now available through Write Bloody Publishing.

Gris Muñoz

Gris Muñoz is a frontera poet and storyteller. She is the author of the bilingual poetry and short story collection *Coatlicue Girl*. Her work has been published in *The Rumpus* and *Bitch Media* among others and she has most recently been featured by Chicana Motherwork, The Tamarindo Podcast, and the Latino Collection & Resource Center at San Antonio Public Library in collaboration with Texas Public Radio. Gris is currently commissioned to write the biography of acclaimed LA artist Fabian Debora. She is Xicana of Apache descent.

Joshua Nguyen

Joshua Nguyen is a Vietnamese-American writer, a collegiate national poetry slam champion (CUPSI), and a native Houstonian. He is the author of the chapbook *American Lục Bát for My Mother* (forthcoming, 2021), published by Bull City Press, and has received fellowships from Kundiman, Sundress Academy For The Arts, and the Vermont Studio Center. He has been published in *The Offing, Wildness, American Poetry Review, The Texas Review, Auburn Avenue, Crab Orchard Review*, and *Gulf Coast Mag*. He has also been featured on both the "VS" podcast and Tracy K. Smith's, "The Slowdown". He is a bubble tea connoisseur and works in a kitchen. He is a PhD student at The University of Mississippi, where he also received his MFA.

Naomi Shihab Nye

Naomi Shihab Nye graduated from Trinity University in San Antonio, TX. She is on faculty at Texas State University and is the Young People's Poet Laureate of the United States (Poetry Foundation).

Amalia Ortiz

Tejana poet and playwright Amalia Ortiz appeared on three seasons of *Russell Simmons Presents Def Poetry on HBO*. NBC Latino named her book, *Rant. Chant. Chisme.* one of "10 Great Latino Books of 2015." It won the 2015 Writers' League of Texas Poetry Discovery Prize. Amalia was chosen to speak at TEDx McAllen 2015. She was awarded an Alfredo

Cisneros Del Moral Grant and a writing residency at the National Hispanic Cultural Center. She is a CantoMundo Fellow, a Hedgebrook writer-in-residence alumna, and she was the inaugural performing-artist-in-residence at ArtPace in 2018. She was awarded a NALAC Fund for the Arts Grant to film music videos for her latest book *The Canción Cannibal Cabaret* (Aztlan Libre Press). In 2020, She won the American Book Award for Oral Literature. Amalia received her MFA in Creative Writing from The University of Texas Rio Grande Valley.

Emmy Pérez

Emmy Pérez, Texas Poet Laureate 2020, has lived in the Texas borderlands for the past 20 years, the first six in El Paso where she has family roots before she moved to McAllen where she currently lives. She is the author of the poetry collections *With the River on Our Face* (University of Arizona Press) and *Solstice* (Swan Scythe Press). A volume of her New and Selected poems is forthcoming from TCU Press.

Octavio Quintanilla

Born in Harlingen, TX, and having lived in Mexico till the age of nine, Octavio Quintanilla, Ph.D. has resided in San Antonio since the fall of 2013 when he began teaching in the MA/MFA program at Our Lady of the Lake University.

Octavio is the author of the poetry collection *If I Go Missing* (Slough Press, 2014). His poetry, fiction, translations, and photography have appeared, or are forthcoming, in journals such as *Salamander, RHINO, Alaska Quarterly Review, Pilgrimage, The Texas Observer*, and others.

Joshua Robbins

Joshua Robbins is the author of *Praise Nothing* (U of Arkansas P, 2013), part of the Miller Williams Series in Poetry, and his recognitions include the James Wright Poetry Award, the New South Prize, selection for Best New Poets, and a Walter E. Dakin Fellowship in poetry from the Sewanee Writers' Conference. He teaches creative writing at the University of the Incarnate Word and lives in San Antonio.

Lacey Roop

Lacey Roop is a nationally touring spoken word artist who has previously ranked 6th in the world at the Women of the World Poetry Slam, featured on PBS's highly acclaimed show, Roadtrip Nation, which reaches 60 million households worldwide, and has performed alongside other notable artists such as the Grammy-Award winning band, The Wailers. Their work is widely considered both engaging and inspiring as it focuses on LGBTQ+ issues, gender and racial equality, environmentalism, intersectionality and on trying to make the world a better place for all.

Amir Safi

Amir Safi is a writer from College Station and is based out of Houston. He is the founder of Write About Now and his work has been featured by The Huffington Post, Upworthy, A plus, Whataburger and more. Most recently, he won the Poetry International Prize.

Andrea "Vocab" Sanderson

Andrea "Vocab" Sanderson is a San Antonio native that's been performing for over twenty years. She serves as a Teaching Artist for Gemini Ink since 2009. Sanderson is the winner of the 2019 People's Choice Award Luminaria Artist Foundation, and a 2020 recipient of the Friends of San Antonio Public Library Arts and Letters Award. Her debut book is entitled *She Lives in Music*, Flower Song Press 2020. Her album *She Tastes like Music* is available on all music streaming platforms. On April 1st 2020, Andrea became the first African American, Poet Laureate of San Antonio 2020-2023. You can find her online at www.andreavocabsanderson.com and IG: Vocabulous

Shaggy

In 2016, Shaggy co-wrote, co-directed, co-produced, and co-starred in *American Pride*, an anti-war play performed in San Antonio, i.e. Military City. During the second performance, an angry audience member stormed out. Five months later, *American Pride* won two Alamo Theatre

Arts Council awards for Overall Production of a Drama and Overall Writing for a Drama. The audience member who stormed out was one of the judges, and that is San Antonio in a nutshell.

Sip

I am a deep dirty southern breed native. I try to write stories to remind myself where I came from and where I wanna be. Use whatever pronoun is gonna make you remember God made both of us.

Ebony Stewart

Ebony Stewart is an international touring poet and performance artist. Her work speaks to the black experience, with emphasis on gender, sexuality, womanhood, and race, with the hopes to be relatable, remove shame, heal minds, encourage dialogue, and inspire folks in marginalized communities. As one of the most decorated poets in Texas, Ebony is a respected coach & mentor, one of the top touring poets in the country, and a Woman of the World Poetry Slam Champion.

The Sexual Health activist and former Sex Educator is also pursuing a license as a Sex Therapist. As a playwright, Ebony's one woman shows, *Hunger* and *Ocean* have received B. Iden Payne Awards & the David Mark Cohen New Play Award.

She is the author of *Love Letters to Balled Fists* and *Home.Girl.Hood.* Her work has been featured in *For Harriet*, *AfroPunk*, *Teen Vogue*, and *The Texas Observer*. The only poet to perform at the 2018 Seattle Pride Festival before 200,000 people, was Ebony Stewart.

She is, #thestoryoftheblackgirlwinning

Danny Strack

Danny Strack (:Dny) is a writer, artist, juggler, and performance poet with a poetry slam career spanning over fifteen years. He's got a few championship titles at national and regional level slams and served as Slammaster of the Austin Poetry Slam from 2010-2015. Danny has written two plays, twelve original books of poetry and a whole lot of marketing material over the years. :Dny is happy to be alive.

Natalia Treviño

Born in Mexico, Natalia is the author of *VirginX* (Finishing Line Press) and has won several awards for her writing including the Alfredo Cisneros del Moral Award, the Dorothy Sargent Rosenberg Poetry Prize, the Literary Award from the Artist Foundation of San Antonio, and the Menada Literary Award at the Ditet e Naimet Poetry Festival in Macedonia. Her first full length collection of poetry, *Lavando La Dirty Laundry* (Mongrel Empire Press) was a finalist for the International Rubery Award and The Writers League of Texas Poetry Award. Natalia graduated from UTSA and the University of Nebraska at Omaha's MFA program. She is a Professor of English at Northwest Vista College. Her publications appear in *The Southern Poetry Anthology, Mirrors Beneath the Earth* (Curbstone Press), *Bordersenses, Borderlands Texas Poetry Review, Sugar House Review, The Taos Journal of Poetry and Art*, and several other journals and anthologies.

Jomar Valentin

Jomar Valentin is a LGBTQIA+ artist based in Austin, TX. Originally from the Philippines, his family immigrated to the United States in 2001 and settled in South Texas. He then moved to Austin, TX in 2007 to attend The University of Texas at Austin.

With over a decade of experience as a spoken word artist, Valentin has repeatedly represented teams Austin Neo Soul & Austin Poetry slam on National stages since 2009. His work focuses on his lived experience as a gay man, and as a first-generation immigrant often utilizing Tagalog (Filipino) words and phrases in his pieces. His poems have been published in *Hothouse* and in anthologies published by 310 Brown Street. His work has been featured on Button Poetry, WAN Poetry, & the Poetry Slam Inc. YouTube Channel.

In 2015, Valentin was named the Slam Master of the renowned Austin Poetry Slam, becoming the first and only POC & LGBTQIA+ individual to occupy the position since the organization's formation in 1994. He is a current resident of East Austin.

Viktoria Valenzuela

Viktoria Valenzuela is a Zoeglossia Fellow, Macondista, and the organizer of 100 Thousand Poets for Change San Antonio. She is a currently earning her MA-MFA in creative writing and social justice at Our Lady of the Lake University. Her poetry can be read in *We Are Not Your Metaphor: A Disability Poetry Anthology*, *Puro Chicanx Writers of the 21st Century*, and *Mutha Magazine*.

Alexandra van de Kamp

Alexandra van de Kamp is the Executive Director for Gemini Ink, San Antonio's Writing Arts Center. Her most recent books of poems are *Kiss/Hierarchy* (Rain Mountain Press 2016) and *The Park of Upside-Down Chairs* (CW Books 2010). She has also published several chapbooks, including *A Liquid Bird Inside the Night* (Red Glass Books 2015) and *Dear Jean Seberg* (2011), which won the 2010 Burnside Review Chapbook Contest. Her poems have been published in journals nationwide, such as *The Texas Observer*, *The Cincinnati Review*, *Denver Quarterly*, *Washington Square*, *32Poems*, *San Antonio Express-News* and more. She is currently at work on a third manuscript of poems.

Eddie Vega

Eddie Vega is a poet, spoken word artist, and educator originally from the Rio Grande Valley of South Texas, currently residing in San Antonio. His poetry has been displayed on VIA Buses and downtown San Antonio buildings. In 2017, he was the runner-up in the Haiku Death Match at the National Poetry Slam. His first full-length collection of poetry *Chicharra Chorus* was published in 2019 by FlowerSong Press. He is a co-host of the Words and Sh*t podcast. Vega writes about food, Tejano culture, social justice, and the intersections thereof. Known as the Taco-Poet of Texas, he can be found at an open-mic, slam, or taqueria on any given non-quarantine evening anywhere throughout South Texas.

Texas Poets Speak Out 161

Edward Vidaurre

Edward Vidaurre is the author of seven collections of poetry. His new book of poems is *Pandemia & Other Poems* (Aztlan Libre Press, 2020). He is the 2018-2019 City of McAllen, Texas Poet Laureate, a four-time Pushcart-nominated poet, and publisher of FlowerSong Press. His writings have appeared or are forthcoming in *The New York Times*, *The Texas Observer*, *Grist*, *Poet Lore*, *The Acentos Review*, *Poetrybay*, *Voices de la Luna*, as well as other journals and anthologies. Vidaurre resides in McAllen, Texas with his wife and daughter.

Buddy Wakefield

Buddy Wakefield is an actor, writer, producer, and three-time world champion spoken word artist featured on the BBC, HBO's *Def Poetry Jam*, ABC *Radio National* and has been signed to both Sage Francis' Strange Famous Records as well as Ani DiFranco's Righteous Babe Records. In 2004 he won the first Individual World Poetry Slam Finals thanks to the support of anthropologist and producer Norman Lear, then went on to share the stage with nearly every notable performance poet in the world in over 2000 venues internationally from The Great Lawn of Central Park, Zimbabwe's Shoko Festival and Scotland's Oran Mor to San Quentin State Penitentiary, House of Blues New Orleans and The Basement in Sydney, Australia.

He is the founder of Awful Good Writers, and the producer and host of *Heavy Hitters Festival 2020*, a summer-long series of online shows and workshops featuring thirty of the most beloved performance poets alive. The inaugural author released on Write Bloody Publishing, and an original Board of Directors member with Youth Speaks Seattle, Buddy is published in dozens of books internationally with work used to win multiple national collegiate debate and forensics competitions. His first short film, *Farmly*, directed by Jamie DeWolf, won Best of Texas at the Literally Short Film Fest, and the USA Film Festival.

Wakefield, who is not concerned with what poetry is or is not, delivers raw, rounded, disarming performances of humor and heart. He is now based in Los Angeles, CA, where he lives as a free agent pursuing acting and screenwriting for both television and film.

Paul Wilkinson Jr.

Paul Wilkinson Jr. is a co-founder of The Blah Poetry Spot. He currently serves as chairman of the board for Write Art Out, a literary non-profit that serves the San Antonio writers community. As a poet, he has performed throughout the United States and Dubai/Abu Dhabi. He published his first book *Underground Kings* which was a fundraiser for several homeless shelters in San Antonio and Atlanta. He is the co-owner of Black America Clothing Co., co-host of the *Horribly Good Guys* podcast, and host of several live music events in the area.

RJ Wright

RJ Wright, is a writer from Seattle, Washington, by way of Cambridge, England. He has a BS in psychology with a minor in military science from The Prairie View A&M University. He is now pursuing a Masters in Human Science and serving as a First Lieutenant in the United States Army Reserve, currently living in Houston TX. He hopes to inspire a new generation of writers and poets as well as promote mental health in the African American community through his art.

Sherrie "Candy" Zantea

Sherrie Zantea (Candy) has been writing and performing poetry for over 26 years. Candy made the 2007 Dallas Poetry Slam Team, and to date has been on 13 poetry slam teams, the first woman to coach 8 and she is the current CEO of the Dallas Poetry Slam Organization. Candy is one of the Lead Instructors for the Literary Arts in the DFW School Districts. She recently created a teaching artist program for Dallas Poetry Slam that partners with youth organizations in the country. Candy is the current Program Director for The Writer's Garret which is a Learning Partner for Big Thought Youth Development Non-Profit and the Dallas Independent School District as well as other school districts in the surrounding areas. In addition to her poetry slam experience, she has added to her resume, Host City Coordinator for 3 Women of the World Poetry Slam Competitions, 2020 International Team Poetry Slam and the Individual World Poetry Slam. She continues to organize events throughout the country. Candy was a speaker at the inaugural TedxFrisco 2020. She maintains a lucrative partnership with WordSpace Non-Profit literacy organization. Candy facilitates workshops with schools and universities across the county. Candy has published a poetry/recipe book *Heirlooms*, a spiritual chap book, *Sherrie's Sanctuary*, her upcoming project *Oak Cliff-Hangers, Stories from a Snowglobe* is set to be released August 2020.

Joaquín Zihuatanejo

Joaquín Zihuatanejo was awarded the 2017 Anhinga Press-Robert Dana Prize for Poetry. His latest collection, Arsonist, was published by Anhinga Press in September of 2018. His work has been featured in *Prairie Schooner, Sonora Review, Huizache,* and *Southwestern American Literature* among other journals and anthologies. Joaquín received his MFA from the Institute of American Indian Arts in Santa Fe, New Mexico. His work has been featured on NBC, HBO, and NPR in *Historias* and *The National Teachers Initiative*. Joaquín has two passions in his life, his partner Aída and poetry, always in that order.

Editors' Bios

C.L. "Rooster" Martinez

Christopher "Rooster" Martinez is a writer and spoken word poet from San Antonio, Texas. he earned a MA/MFA from the Creative Writing, Literature and Social Justice program at Our Lady of the Lake University. In 2011, Rooster co-founded the Blah Poetry Spot, a local poetry open mic and community organization. He is a 2-time San Antonio Slam Champion, and part of the team that took 3rd place at the 2017 National Poetry Slam Group Piece Competition. His work has appeared in such publications as Write About Now Poetry, Button Poetry, The Huffington Post Latino Voices, *Pilgrimage Press*, and *Acentos Review*. He has two books, *A Saint for Lost Things*, from Alabrava Press, and *As it is in Heaven*, from Kissing Dynamite Poetry Press.

M.R. "Chibbi" Orduña

Chibbi is a Mexican-born, Texas-raised queer poet and actor. He is the founder of Laredo BorderSlam, a founding member of Write About Now, the co-host of the *Words and Sh*t* podcast, and 2-time San Antonio Slam Champion, winning 3rd place at the 2017 National Poetry Slam Group Piece Competition. He has self-published 2 books; his latest *OTRO/PATRIA* was released in the summer of 2019. His work primarily deals with the exploration of identity and culture, his experiences as both Queer and Latino, and fighting for the validity of existence. He has toured across the country performing his spoken word sets, and his work has been featured in the Houston LGBTQIA magazine *OutSmart*, and published in the 2017 Anthology *Best Emerging Poets in Texas*, the 2020 *Latino Book Review Magazine*, and online on We Are Mitu, George Takei, SlamFind, Poetry Slam Inc, Button Poetry, and Write About Now. You can follow his adventures on IG @gemineyes and get more info at www.gemineyespoetry.com.

www.ingramcontent.com/pod-product-compliance
Lightning Source LLC
Chambersburg PA
CBHW071241070526
44583CB00017B/2278